POPULATION & HUMAN SURVIVAL

IDEAS in CONFLICT

Gary E. McCuen

GEM GARY McCUEN
publications inc.

411 Mallalieu Drive
Hudson, Wisconsin 54016
Phone (715) 386-7113

Illustrations & Photo Credits

Eleanor Bader 114, Locher 11, Ron Swanson 27, 89, 95, 119, Sam Scrawls 82, 100, David Seavey 20, U.S. Senate Committee on Foreign Affairs 34, 109, USA Today 46, Zero Population Growth 52, 67, 142

© 1993 By Gary E. McCuen Publications, Inc.
411 Mallalieu Drive, Hudson, Wisconsin 54016

publications inc. (715) 386-7113

International Standard Book Number
0-86596-089-5 Printed in the United States
of America

CONTENTS

REASONING SKILL DEVELOPMENT

The following activities may be used as individualized study guides for students in libraries and resource centers or as discussion catalysts in small group and classroom discussions.

This series features ideas in conflict on political, social, and moral issues. It presents counterpoints, debates, opinions, commentary, and analysis for use in libraries and classrooms. Each title in the series uses one or more of the following basic elements:

Introductions *that present an issue overview giving historic background and/or a description of the controversy.*

Counterpoints *and debates carefully chosen from publications, books, and position papers on the political right and left to help librarians and teachers respond to requests that treatment of public issues be fair and balanced.*

Symposiums *and forums that go beyond debates that can polarize and oversimplify. These present commentary from across the political spectrum that reflect how complex issues attract many shades of opinion.*

A **global** *emphasis with foreign perspectives and surveys on various moral questions and political issues that will help readers to place subject matter in a less culture-bound and ethnocentric frame of reference. In an ever-shrinking and interdependent world, understanding and cooperation are essential. Many issues are global in nature and can be effectively dealt with only by common efforts and international understanding.*

Reasoning skill *study guides and discussion activities provide ready-made tools for helping with critical reading and evaluation of content. The guides and activities deal with one or more of the following:*

RECOGNIZING AUTHOR'S POINT OF VIEW

INTERPRETING EDITORIAL CARTOONS

VALUES IN CONFLICT

WHAT IS EDITORIAL BIAS?

WHAT IS SEX BIAS?

WHAT IS POLITICAL BIAS?

WHAT IS ETHNOCENTRIC BIAS?

WHAT IS RACE BIAS?

WHAT IS RELIGIOUS BIAS?

From across **the political spectrum** *varied sources are presented for research projects and classroom discussions. Diverse opinions in the series come from magazines, newspapers, syndicated columnists, books, political speeches, foreign nations, and position papers by corporations and nonprofit institutions.*

About the Editor

Gary E. McCuen is an editor and publisher of anthologies for public libraries and curriculum materials for schools. Over the past years his publications have specialized in social, moral and political conflict. They include books, pamphlets, cassettes, tabloids, filmstrips and simulation games, many of them designed from his curriculums during 11 years of teaching junior and senior high school social studies. At present he is the editor and publisher of the *Ideas in Conflict* series and the *Editorial Forum* series.

CHAPTER 1

THE GLOBAL POPULATION CRISIS: AN OVERVIEW

1 THE GLOBAL POPULATION CRISIS: AN OVERVIEW

THE POPULATION DEBATE: COMPETING THEORIES

Peter Stalker

Peter Stalker is a co-editor of the New Internationalist, *a Canadian magazine dealing with world affairs.*

Points to Consider:

1. Who are the Malthusians?

2. How do developmentalists view population growth?

3. Describe the ideology of the New Right toward population control.

4. What happened at the Mexico City Conference in 1984?

Peter Stalker, "Malthus and Morality," New Internationalist, October 1987.

The man usually credited with starting the whole population ball rolling was an Englishman, Thomas Malthus.

In August 1986, the U.S. Agency for International Development (USAID) withheld all funding from UNFPA (United Nations Fund for Population Activities). It isn't so long ago that the advocates of population control were being attacked not from the right but from the left. Family planners used to be condemned as lackeys of U.S. imperialism who wanted to suppress the dark threatening hordes of the Third World poor.

The Malthusians

A bit of history might shed some light. The man usually credited with starting the whole population ball rolling was an Englishman, Thomas Malthus. In his *Essay on Population* in 1803, he was the first person to consider what would happen if the world's population were to continue to grow unabated. Like plants that jostle for a bare minimum of soil and light, human beings would eventually fill all the available territory, he warned.

True to his predictions, the population of Europe and North America did indeed grow dramatically in the 150 years that followed. But, contrary to his expectations, his gloomy prognosis was disproved. Human beings turned out to be more intelligent than dandelions and modified their behavior to match the new circumstances. Parents in the new cities, with their clean water and sewage systems, found their healthy offspring more expensive to feed, clothe and educate so they decided, without the help of any population policy, to limit the size of their families.

Life in the poorer countries remained dangerous and short, however, with disease continuing to take its regular toll of young children. But after World War II, health and sanitation started to improve there, too. Soon the Malthusian spectre rose up again as populations soared.

Changing Times

But the Sixties were an optimistic decade. For every problem there was a technical solution. And the technical solution to the population problem was contraception. So Western experts were soon jetting off to poor countries to run surveys and design massive family-planning programs. And when these didn't meet with immediate success, yet more surveys were done and more

10

Locher, **Chicago Tribune**. Reprinted by permission: **Tribune Media Services**

programs developed—until, ultimately, it was decided that, if parents could not be trusted to do the right thing, the decision had to be taken out of their hands. Helicopters dropped experts into unsuspecting villages in Nepal; Tunisian women were coerced into buses to have loops inserted without explanation; African women were given contraceptive injections against their or their husbands' will.

Not surprisingly this produced a strong counter-reaction. Radical voices in developing countries began to accuse the West of plotting to keep down the numbers in the Third World so as to maintain their own privileged position. Come the Seventies, it was time for a rethink. Some of the experts investigated further. They discovered that people in poor countries persisted in having so many children because they wanted them. The reason seemed to be that the improvements in sanitation and health in Europe and North America had occurred alongside general economic progress. Parents with higher incomes had less need of child labor. So children turned from an asset into a liability and, in academic parlance, a "demographic transition" took place as high rates of death and

11

birth were replaced by low ones.

Competing Theories

In poor countries, however, incomes did not rise as death rates began to fall. So parents actually welcomed the possibility of a large family; an extra pair of hands could soon pay for itself by working in the fields as well as ensuring security for the parents' old age.

So a new population wisdom emerged: only when people were financially secure could they risk smaller families. Once they were better off they would start using contraceptives of their own accord. "Take care of the people and the population will take care of itself" was their slogan. If you like labels, you could call this new group the "developmentalists."

By 1974 — year of the first ever World Population Conference in Bucharest — there were roughly three population camps. In the first were the **Malthusians.** Led by U.S. Agency for International Development (USAID), they argued that people in the Third World were poor because they were having too many children. This position received support from an emerging environmental movement and an influential new report — *Limits to Growth* from the Club of Rome — which warned that the world was running out of oil and almost everything else. The second camp was inhabited largely by a group of **skeptical, defensive Third World governments**, who often refused to consider that they had a population problem at all. In the third camp — implicitly supporting the Third World position — were the **developmentalists**, which included the United Nations Fund for Population Activities (UNFPA). They argued that development would eventually take the Third World through its own demographic transition to low rates of death and birth.

In the years that followed, the developmentalists turned out to have most of the evidence on their side. This forced even the most raucous Malthusian pill-pushers to tone down their rhetoric and "integrate" family planning into health and development programs.

However, some Third World governments also started to shift their approach — often, ironically, towards a more Malthusian position. These *nouveau-riches* elites were getting worried about the increasing numbers of poor families camped outside their large houses. And some of the worst excesses during this period came from Third World governments, such as Sanjay Ghandi's notorious sterilization campaign in India in 1976.

Later still, both Malthusians and developmentalists softened their lines. The Malthusians now had their "integrated" health programs, albeit only thinly disguised family-planning campaigns. But the developmentalists, too, were having second thoughts. A massive 42-country World Fertility Survey, commissioned by UNFPA and USAID, demonstrated that half the women who wanted no more children had no access to contraception. So distribution of information and contraceptives was now accepted as a way of meeting this "unmet need", alongside other development efforts.

Other Forces

But just as these two groups began moving closer together, other forces were gathering which threatened to blow the consensus wide apart once more.

The first new force was the **women's movement** (always prominent in the field of family planning, but now with more international influence). Now, much of what they were saying—particularly their insistence that women had a right to control their bodies and therefore a right to family planning—was welcomed by all sides of the population industry. But the feminists went further. They argued that the right to control their own bodies should include the right to abortion. This outraged the Catholic Church of course. But this was nothing new. What was new was the uproar this caused among the second new force on the population scene—the **New Right.**

The New Right—in the guise of the Reagan Administration in the U.S. and, to a lesser extent, Thatcherism in the UK—had already attacked most of the conventional developmentalist wisdom of the Seventies. Aid was discredited, as was the whole idea of development planning. Third World governments should be stepping aside and letting market forces work their magic, they argued. Now they went to work on population, too.

New Right population ideology has two distinct components: the **economic** and the **moral.** The high priest on the **economic front** is Professor Julian Simon of the University of Maryland. For him more people are not a problem: on the contrary, they are the "ultimate resource". Providing they are not restrained by government interference, newly-born humans offer a fresh source of ingenuity and can provide solutions to many more problems than they cause—by discovering new energy sources, for instance. The **moral component** of the New Right's population ideology, on the other hand, is based upon the sanctity of family life and the rights of the fetus. It is resolutely opposed to abortion and would like to see women firmly back in the home.

13

Mexico City

In fact, there is no logical connection between the moral and economic components—Simon himself is not against abortion. What ties them together was their adoption by the Reagan Administration, which used Simon's economic thesis to give intellectual backbone to their moralistic assertions. But put together, they produced a potent brew which caused an extraordinary about-face in U.S. government policy: at the 1984 World Population Conference in Mexico City, the U.S. described population growth as merely a "neutral phenomenon". The real problem, they argued, was government interference in the efficient play of market forces.

But it was the moral part of the New Right's package that really put the cat among the pigeons. On grounds that they were funding programs which included abortion, the U.S. cut off its support to UNFPA. The International Planned Parenthood Federation—an association of local family planning organizations around the world—also lost its U.S. funding because it would not promise to deny women the option of an abortion.

So now the ideological battlefield is littered with a number of often overlapping forces, Malthusians, feminists and developmentalists, as well as the moralists and economists of the New Right. And you are likely to find representatives of all camps within any given organization. Now that you have an idea of what is going on, you could be forgiven for throwing up your hands in disgust and letting them all get on with it. The Third World poor, on the receiving end of programs designed by one faction or the other, do not have this option.

EXAMINING ISSUES OF MORALITY AND SOCIAL JUSTICE

This activity may be used as an individualized study guide for students in libraries and resource centers or as a discussion catalyst in small group and classroom discussions.

Issues of morality and social justice are usually complex and often incorporate views from many diverse cultural, religious, national, economic, political and personal backgrounds. Population control and family size is a very personal matter for most citizens of the world and suggestions to limit reproductive behavior create much controversy.

PART ONE

Listed below are the five major categories of opinion on the issue of population control as outlined in Reading One. Review this reading and write a brief description of each position listed.

A. MALTHUSIAN

B. DEVELOPMENTALIST

C. FEMINIST

NEW RIGHT:

D. ECONOMIC

E. MORALIST

PART TWO

1. What category or position do you agree with the most? Why?

2. Read each statement below and match it to one (or more) of the five categories listed in Part One of this activity. Mark each statement with the appropriate letter(s).

___Population control has historically had its roots in a militaristic view of the world that sees a shrinking West increasingly outnumbered by rapidly growing nations of the Third World.

___It's time for the U.S. to regain the moral high ground for effective family planning in the Third World.

___Birth rate is not only affected by biological factors such as fertility and contraception, but by equally powerful social factors.

___America's affluent, well-educated citizens contribute far more to the population crisis than do people of developing nations.

___Poor women are much more likely to die from pregnancy than from contraceptive side effects.

___Population controllers are motivated by sectarian self-interests tinged with racism.

___Uncontrolled population growth in subsistence economies is degrading the resource base throughout Africa.

___The security of the industrial nations depends, in part, on the management of populations in the Third World.

___In terms of population density, Africa is actually underpopulated.

CHAPTER 2

DEBATING POPULATION GROWTH

2   DEBATING POPULATION GROWTH

THE POPULATION "EXPLOSION" IS A SERIOUS THREAT

Paul R. Ehrlich and Anne H. Ehrlich

Paul Ehrlich is Bing Professor of Population Studies at Stanford University and a member of the National Academy of Sciences. Anne Ehrlich is a senior biology researcher, also at Stanford, and author of several books on the environment. This essay is from their book, The Population Explosion.

Points to Consider:

1. What is meant by exponential growth?

2. What will be the consequences of uncontrolled population growth?

3. How do the authors view the Catholic Church's position?

4. Why is population a "taboo" for serious discussion?

Paul R. Ehrlich and Anne H. Ehrlich, "The Population Explosion", **The Amicus Journal,** Winter 1990.

Nature may end the population explosion for us—in very unpleasant ways.

In the early 1930s, when we were born, the world population was just two billion; now it is more than two-and-a-half times as large and still growing rapidly.

A Slow Trend

Our own species, *Homo sapiens,* evolved a few hundred thousand years ago. Some ten thousand years ago, when agriculture was invented, probably no more than five million people inhabited Earth – fewer than now live in the San Francisco Bay Area. Even at the time of Christ, two thousand years ago, the entire human population was roughly the size of the population of the United States today; by 1650 there were only 500 million people, and in 1850 only a little over a billion. Since there are now well past five billion people, the vast majority of the population explosion has taken place in less than a tenth of one percent of the history of *Homo sapiens.*

This is a remarkable change in the abundance of a single species. After an unhurried pace of growth over most of our history, expansion of the population accelerated during the Industrial Revolution and really shot up after 1950. Since mid-century, the human population has been growing at annual rates ranging from about 1.7 to 2.1 percent per year, doubling in forty years or less.

But even the highest growth rates are still slow-motion changes compared to events we easily notice and react to. A car swerving at us on the highway is avoided by actions taking a few seconds. The Alaskan oil spill caused great public indignation, but faded from the media and the consciousness of most people in a few months. In four years, the world population expands only a little more than seven percent. Who could notice that? Precipitous as the population explosion has been in historical terms, it is occurring at a snail's pace in an individual's perception. It is not an event; it is a trend that must be analyzed in order for its significance to be appreciated.

Exponential Growth

The time it takes a population to double in size is a dramatic way to picture rates of population growth, one that most of us can understand more readily than percentage growth rates. Human populations have often grown "exponentially".

A classic example used to illustrate this is the pond weed that doubles each day the amount of pond surface covered and is projected to cover the entire pond in thirty days. Just half the pond will be covered in 29 days. The weed will then double once more and cover the entire pond the next day. As this example indicates, exponential growth contains the potential for big surprises.

The limits to human population growth are more difficult to perceive than those restricting the pond weed's growth. Nonetheless, like the pond weed, human populations grow in a pattern that is essentially exponential, so we must be alert to the treacherous properties of that sort of growth. The key point to remember is that a long history of exponential growth in no way implies a long future of exponential growth. What begins in slow motion may eventually overwhelm us in a flash.

The last decade or two has seen a slight slackening in the human population growth rate—a slackening that has been prematurely heralded as an "end to the population explosion". But even if birth rates continue to fall, the world population will continue to expand (assuming that death rates don't rise), although at a slowly slackening rate, for about another century. Demographers think that growth will not end before the population has reached 10 billion or more.

So, even though birth rates have declined somewhat, *Homo sapiens* is a long way from ending its population explosion or avoiding its consequences. In fact, the biggest jump from five to 10 billion in well under a century is still ahead. But this does not mean that growth couldn't be ended sooner, with a much smaller population size, if we—all of the world's nations—made up our minds to do it. The trouble is, many of the world's leaders and perhaps most of the world's people still do not believe that there are compelling reasons to do so. They are even less aware that if humanity fails to act, nature may end the population explosion for us—in very unpleasant ways—well before 10 billion is reached.

Unpleasant Endings

Those unpleasant ways are beginning to be perceptible. Humanity in the 1990s will be confronted by more and more intransigent environmental problems, global problems dwarfing those that worried us in the late 1960s. Perhaps the most serious is global warming, a problem caused in large part by population growth and overpopulation. In addition to more frequent and more severe crop failures, projected consequences of the warming include coastal flooding, desertification, the creation of as many as 300 million environmental refugees, alteration of patterns of disease, water shortages, placing of general stress on natural ecosystems, and other negative interactions among all these factors.

Continued population growth and the drive for development in already badly overpopulated poor nations will make it exceedingly difficult to slow the greenhouse warming—and impossible to stop or reverse it—in this generation at least. And, even if the warming should miraculously not occur, contrary to accepted projections, human members are on a collision course with massive famines anyway.

Global warming, acid rain, depletion of the ozone layer,

vulnerability to epidemics, and exhaustion of soils and groundwater are all related to population size. They are also clear and present dangers to the persistence of civilization. Crop failures due to global warming alone might result in the premature deaths of a billion or more people in the next few decades, and the AIDS epidemic could slaughter hundreds of millions. Together these would constitute a harsh "population control" program provided by nature in the face of humanity's refusal to put into place a gentler program of its own.

We should not delude ourselves: the population explosion will come to an end before very long. The only remaining question is whether it will be halted through the humane method of birth control, or by nature wiping out the surplus. We realize that religious and cultural opposition to birth control exists throughout the world, but people simply do not understand the choice that such opposition implies. Today, anyone opposing birth control is unknowingly voting to have the human population size controlled by a massive increase in early deaths.

Not Just a "Catholic Problem"

Even though the media occasionally give coverage to

population issues, some people never get the word. In 1988, Pope John Paul II reaffirmed the Catholic Church's ban on contraception. The occasion was the twentieth anniversary of Pope Paul's anti-birth control encyclical, *Humanae Vitae.*

Fortunately, the majority of Catholics in the industrial world pay little attention to the encyclical or the Church's official ban on all practical means of birth control. One need only note that Catholic Italy at present has the smallest average completed family size (1.3 children per couple) of any nation.

We wish to emphasize that the population problem is in no sense a "Catholic problem". Around the world, Catholic reproductive performance is much the same as that of non-Catholics in similar cultures and with similar economic status. Nevertheless, the political position of the Vatican, traceable in no small part to the extreme conservatism of Pope John Paul II, is an important barrier to solving the population problem. Non-Catholics should be very careful not to confuse Catholics or Catholicism with the Vatican. Furthermore, the Church's position on contraception is distressing to many millions of Catholics, who feel it morally imperative to follow their own conscience and disregard the Vatican's teachings on this subject in their personal lives.

Nor is unwillingness to face the severity of the population problem limited to the Vatican. It is built into our genes and our culture. That is one reason many otherwise bright and humane people behave like fools when confronted with demographic issues. Thus, an economist specializing in mail-order marketing can sell the thesis that the human population could increase essentially forever because people are the "ultimate resource", and a journalist can urge more population growth in the United States so that we can have a bigger army! Even some environmentalists are taken in by the frequent assertion that "there is no population problem, only a problem of distribution." The statement is usually made in the context of a plan for conquering hunger, as if food shortage were the only consequence of overpopulation.

Food and Hunger

But even in that narrow context, the assertion is wrong. Suppose food were distributed equally. If everyone in the world ate as Americans do, less than half the present world population could be fed on the record harvests of 1985 and 1986. Of course, everyone does not have to eat like Americans. About a third of the world grain harvest — the staples of the human

23

feeding base—is fed to animals to produce eggs, milk and meat for American-style diets. Would not feeding that grain directly to people solve the problem? If everyone were willing to eat an essentially vegetarian diet, that additional grain would allow perhaps a billion more people to be fed with 1986 production.

Taboo

The average person, even the average scientist, seldom makes the connection between seemingly unrelated events and the population problem, and thus remains unworried. To a degree, this failure to put the pieces together is due to a taboo against frank discussion of the population crisis in many quarters, a taboo generated partly by other groups who are afraid that dealing with population issues will produce socially damaging results.

Many people on the political left are concerned that focusing on overpopulation will divert attention from crucial problems of social justice (which certainly need to be addressed in addition to the population problem). Often those on the political right fear that dealing with overpopulation will encourage abortion (it need not) or that halting growth will severely damage the economy (it could, if not handled properly). And people of varied political persuasions who are unfamiliar with the magnitude of the population problem believe in a variety of farfetched technological fixes—such as colonizing outer space—that they think will allow the need for regulating the size of the human population to be avoided forever.

All of us naturally lean toward the taboo against dealing with population growth. The roots of our aversion to limiting the size of the human population are as deep and pervasive as the roots of human sexual behavior. Through billions of years of evolution, out-reproducing other members of your population was the name of the game. It is the very basis of natural selection, the driving force of the evolutionary process. Nonetheless, the taboo must be uprooted and discarded.

There is no more time to waste. Human inaction has already condemned hundreds of millions more people to premature deaths from hunger and disease. The population connection must be made in the public mind. Action to end the population explosion and humanely start a gradual population decline must be taken as soon as possible until the birth rate is lowered to slightly below the human death rate. There still may be time to limit the scope of the impending catastrophe, but not much time.

3 DEBATING POPULATION GROWTH

THERE IS NO POPULATION "EXPLOSION"

Michael Fumento

Michael Fumento is the associate editor of the American Economic Foundation *newsletter. This article was written as a review of Paul Ehrlich's book,* The Population Explosion.

Points to Consider:

1. Why does the author feel that the Ehrlichs are "profits of doom"?

2. What connection is there between population and hunger?

3. Why does the author disagree with Malthus? Give an example.

4. How does the author view the Catholic Church's position?

Michael Fumento, "The Profits of Doom", Crisis, February 1991. Reprinted by permission of **Crisis Magazine,** 1511 K Street, NW, Suite 525, Washington, D. C. 20005.

Erlich forecast huge population increases which simply haven't taken place.

Back in 1968, both Paul Ehrlich, an entomologist at Stanford, and Julian Simon, a professor of economics at the University of Illinois at Champaign-Urbana, were disciples of eighteenth century economist Thomas R. Malthus. Malthus claimed that population grows geometrically (2, 4, 8, 16) while food production grows arithmetically (2, 4, 6, 8); hence the world's population would eventually outstrip its food supply and massive famine would result. Ehrlich wrote a book on the subject that applied it to modern conditions.

Profits of Doom

In *The Population Bomb,* Ehrlich wrote:

"The battle to feed all of humanity is over. In the 1970s the world will undergo famines—hundreds of millions of people are going to starve to death in spite of any crash programs embarked on now. At this late date nothing can prevent a substantial increase in the world death rate."

Elsewhere, in what was presented as a plausible scenario of events by the year 2000, Ehrlich had no less than 65 million Americans starving to death. To prevent such a calamity, he suggested that forced sterilization programs and the injection of birth control drugs into water supplies might be necessary.

As we now know, hundreds of millions of people did not starve to death in the 1970s, and to the extent there was starvation, it was the result of flawed political and economic policies, as in the case of the Ethiopian famine of the 1980s.

In 1990, Ehrlich and his wife Anne produced *The Population Explosion.* In it they wrote:

"The Population Bomb warned of impending disaster if the population explosion was not brought under control. Then the fuse was burning; now the population bomb has detonated. One thing seems safe to predict: starvation and epidemic disease will raise death rates over most of the planet."

The latest book, of course, is complete with all the new buzzwords like "global warming" and "ozone layer", but the basic premise is exactly the same: virtually all of man's problems can be laid at the feet of an ever-growing population.

First, a little information, courtesy of the Bureau of the Census's *Statistical Abstract of the United States* and *Historical*

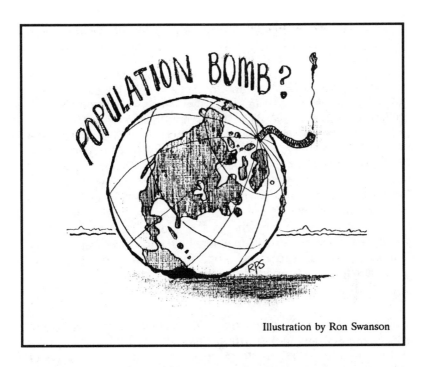

Illustration by Ron Swanson

Statistics of the United States. Food production per person is up, both in the U.S. and the world; likewise for the availability of natural resources as measured by their prices. In the United States, increases have been registered in the cleanliness of air and water, amount of space per person in homes, and most importantly, in the length of life. In fact, Ehrlich could hardly have been more wrong if he had predicted that the nation wouldn't land a man on the moon before the end of the century.

Fallacies

Of all the fallacies in the two Ehrlich population books, two stand out. The first, found primarily in the first book and left unretracted in the second, is that population growth is static. Ignoring the universal trend line—which indicates that as nations become more affluent they tend to breed more slowly—and using outdated figures from an earlier point on the line, Ehrlich forecast huge population increases which simply haven't taken place. In fact, the United States, Japan, and much of Europe are producing children at rates below replacement level, although this condition would have to continue for a few decades for actual net population decreases to show up.

Second, Ehrlich steadfastly embraces Malthusianism which, for the last century, has been proven wrong in fact because it is wrong in theory. Both population growth and food productivity result from a large number of factors, none of which could possibly be reduced to a simple mathematical formula. Indeed, population is utterly irrelevant to the issue of hunger. Instead, there is one simple rule: those countries with collectivist economic systems have difficulty feeding their people; those with capitalist economies do not. Uninterested in this reality, the Ehrlichs make much of one recent year, 1988, in which U.S. crop production actually declined from the previous year and forced the nation to draw on its overflowing storage capacity. What they don't point out is that about one-third of all U.S. crop land lies fallow, pulled out of production by government price support programs. In fact, the root of the entire "farm crisis" (to the extent there is one) is that Malthus and Ehrlich are wrong. The ability to squeeze more crops out of the same amount of land has far outstripped the capacity of the growing human population to consume it. Thus, farmers find it difficult to make a profit.

The Population Explosion may be the ultimate alarmist book. The authors claim that overpopulation is at the root of global warming, rain forest destruction, famine and air and water pollution. AIDS, for example, is one result of overpopulation. Never mind that the Black Death was an incomparably worse epidemic that occurred on a much more sparsely populated planet. Further, only in today's world of "swollen population" has one of the world's greatest pestilences (smallpox) been wiped off the face of the earth.

No More Malthus

1968 was also a watershed year for Julian Simon in that it was his last year as a Malthusian. The next year, he not only became a convert but a missionary.

Simon simply thinks that when it comes to *Homo sapiens*, the more the merrier. About a decade ago he wrote a landmark book, *The Ultimate Resource*, which not only put Ehrlich to shame but made an excellent case, both with words and masses of statistics, charts, and graphs, that the best answer to the problems of humanity lie in the proliferation of free thought, free markets, and human beings free to propagate more or less to their heart's content.

Simon has published a set of his assorted essays, articles, letters, and speeches, put out in conjunction with the Hudson Institute, called *Population Matters*. He looks, for example, at the highly influential 1980 book, *Global 2000 Report to President Jimmy Carter*, which stated that "hundreds of thousands of species—perhaps as many as 20 percent of all species on Earth—will be irretrievably lost as their habitats vanish," and shows that the statement was based on nothing more substantial than an extrapolation from a guess, with no basis in reality. Yet, the claims of some environmental activists that the entire Amazon rain forest will be wiped out at the present rate by the year 2000 stem from the same sort of formula. In fact, actual satellite surveys of rain forest depletion by the UN's Food and Agricultural Organization have shown the rates to be much lower than claimed, although deforestation is a real phenomenon. As to species disappearance, no one really knows its extent, but a good guess would be a one-per-year loss, the same rate we've had for the last 90 years.

The best way to determine the effect of population, notes Simon, is to compare population growth with the standard of living, and both have increased more or less steadily since the beginning of recorded time. For example, even as the population of China was "exploding", its life expectancy in recent decades has risen fully 20 years. In capitalist Hong Kong, one of the most densely populated areas in the world, things have improved even more. "There is no convincing economic reason," he says, "why these trends toward a better life should not continue indefinitely."

The Catholic Church

Simon states that the Catholic church is the best hope for opposition against population control fanaticism. Says Simon:

"Clearly Protestantism does not today urge 'Be fruitful and multiply.' And I was saddened that Judaism does not either. As a non-Catholic, however, I was sure that at least the Roman Catholic is still committed to this belief, and I hope that the Catholic Church would take the lead in promulgating the message about what I consider to be a fundamental tenet of our common religious heritage—that life is good."

He goes on to say, *"The Catholic church seems the only U.S. institution that is committed to the message that more life is good, and to encouraging people to have as many children as they can bring up well."* People-bashing, says Simon, *is not merely a fruitless academic exercise. "This error has cost dearly. It has directed our attention away from the factor that we now know is central in a country's economic development, its economic and political system."*

People Control

Those heaping praise and money on Ehrlich do so not because his arguments are good; they demonstrably are not. They do so because his conclusions are "good".

But why do some people like Ehrlich's conclusions? For two reasons, I suspect. One, many are those who like to control people. They may call themselves "pro-choicers", but don't believe it. Anyone who calls for forced sterilization of human beings isn't pro-choice. These are the self-styled elite, those who believe that the world would be a much better place if they called the shots, that man is perfectible through a proper social system, and that government can be used to establish that social system. Finally, they don't like anything or anybody that falls outside that system.

In a sense, controlling the numbers of people is the ultimate control of people. The second probable motivation is simply a visceral dislike of more people, which is exemplified by a Ziggy T-shirt I once saw. On it, the rotund cartoon figure is featured saying, "I love society; it's people I can't stand." Paul Ehrlich can't stand people, a fact which came across quickly in his 1968 book where he wrote that his thinking had been seriously affected by the sheer mass of humanity he saw on a trip to India.

Said Ehrlich: "The streets seemed alive with people. People eating, people washing, people sleeping. People visiting, arguing and screaming. People thrusting their hands through the taxi windows, begging. People defecating and urinating. People clinging to buses. People herding animals. People,

people, people, people."

Many of the environmental alarmists, including apparently the Ehrlichs, share a romantic view that the best time in history was pre-industrial revolution agrarian society when there were a lot fewer of those *Homo sapiens* around. Never mind that London's famous fog came mostly from wood stoves, that horse excrement caused sickness and death far beyond that caused by air and water pollution, that life in general was nasty, brutish, and short.

About 20 years ago, some of my family watched a television show on how increasing population would bring the world to ruin. My little brother was reduced to tears. He has now survived to the ripe old age of 28 and is living in a world that in most ways is a much better place than it was then. Probably Ehrlich had a hand in that television show, whether directly or merely through inspiration. And without a doubt he will now inspire more such shows and terrify more little boys with logic and reasoning that is most fit for that age group. He has done so well at it that it is almost certainly asking too much of him to switch into a more respectable line of work.

4 DEBATING POPULATION GROWTH

LIFE IS GETTING WORSE

Carl Wahren

Carl Wahren made the following comments as head of the Aid Manage-ment Division of the Organization for Economic Cooperation and Development (OECD).

Points to Consider:

1. What areas have the highest rate of population increase?

2. Why is population growth a threat to agricultural output?

3. How does population adversely affect the environment?

4. How does population growth affect jobs and women in the Third World?

Excerpted from material submitted by Carl Wahren before a hearing of the House Committee on Science, Space and Technology on the Global Food and Population Situation, March 2, 1989.

The World Bank has estimated that some 800 million people now lack enough food to maintain an active working life.

It took until 1927 for the world population to reach two billion. In only 70 years, Third World countries will add some 4.8 billion to their populations to reach 6.6 billion by 2020.

Alarming Figures

Africa's prospects are alarming. The population has risen from 225 million in 1950 to 600 million in 1987. It is projected to reach 880 million by the end of the century and 1.6 billion by 2025. Now 45 percent of the African population is under 15 years of age. In several East African countries, annual rates of increase are 3.5 percent or more, implying a population doubling time of 20 years or less.

Southern Asia will be the most heavily populated region for some decades. Its present population of 1.14 billion (815 million in India) will increase to some 1.5 billion by the year 2000 and reach nearly two billion 20 years later (1.3 billion in India). In Bangladesh, which is already more than twice as densely populated as, say, Belgium, the present population of 105 million is projected to double by 2020.

Most Arab countries have seen little or no lowering of birth rates, whereas crude death rates are relatively low.

When considering the population increase in the South, it should be remembered that today's industrialized countries never experienced anything of that order in their histories. At their peak, during the last century, growth rates in Europe rarely exceeded 1.5 percent. Thus a country like Kenya is now increasing its population almost three times as fast as did European nations at their historical swiftest. Even in North America, the maximum demographic growth rate, boosted by immigration, was only two percent a year, with massive land and natural resources to support it.

Many Third World populations have been rising faster than agricultural output. In about 70 countries, food production per head of population has declined since the 1970s.

Food Falls Behind

Except for Asia, developing countries have had to import an increasing part of their food requirements. An annual cereal deficit of 10 million tons in the mid-1960s rose to 33 million in

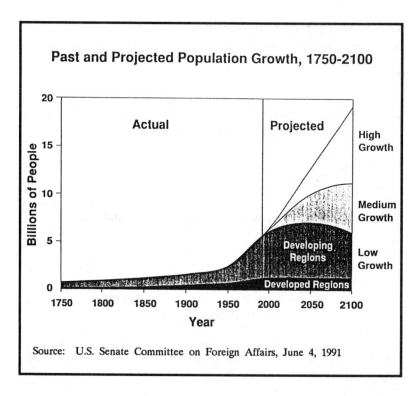

Past and Projected Population Growth, 1750-2100

Actual

Projected

High
Growth

Medium
Growth

Developing
Regions

Low
Growth

Developed Regions

Billions of People

Year

Source: U.S. Senate Committee on Foreign Affairs, June 4, 1991

1975-1979, and on present trends, could reach 132 million tons by the year 2000.

The World Bank has estimated that some 800 million people now lack enough food to maintain an active working life: that is, they survive on below 90 percent of the minimum requirements that have been defined by the Food and Agriculture Organization (FAO) and World Health Organization (WHO). The number of people running serious health risks because of calorie deficiency reached some 340 million in 1980.

Malnutrition hits countries with adequate food supplies, and not just the poorest. There are several explanations: marked social inequalities, very low purchasing power for some categories of the population, and problems of storage and transport. Although the number of malnourished people has declined in the past two decades as a proportion of the world's total, in absolute terms it has risen.

Arable land area is unlikely to increase by more than five percent between now and the year 2000. So most of the extra food required will have to come from higher yields. But these in the main depend heavily on water, oil and fertilizers. And the long-term environmental implications of modern farming techniques are disquieting, particularly in parts of Africa.

Pressure on the Environment

Population pressures overload the capacities of the environment in many developing countries. The momentum of population growth combined with widespread poverty creates serious imbalances between population sizes and the ecosystem.

Some 95 percent of projected increase in the world's population from five billion of today to over six billion by 2000 will take place in developing regions, which are often environmentally fragile. This imbalance will aggravate the problems of poverty and increase the number of environmental refugees. During the 1970s twice as many people suffered from "natural" disasters as in the 1960s, in particular from floods and droughts caused by neglect of the environmental fundamentals. The trends foreseen for the 1990s are no brighter.

Population pressures lead to the increased consumption of natural resources. Drinking water is already becoming scarce as rivers, lakes and oceans are polluted. Countries in desert regions buy themselves varying periods of grace by pumping groundwater out of subterranean pockets. Hydrologists are worried that several countries, particularly in sub-Saharan Africa, may rapidly be approaching acute water shortages. This will not only threaten their growing populations but will undermine their attempts to industrialize and modernize agriculture.

Rapidly growing food and energy requirements caused by high population growth aggravate the alarming trends of desertification and deforestation. Over-grazing by expanding livestock herds and over-cultivation make them even more vulnerable still. According to one UN report, nearly one-third of all land is at risk of turning into desert, and topsoil is being lost at the rate of 26 billion tons a year.

Short-Term Difficulties

Because so many developing countries are in serious economic difficulties, they seize short-term opportunities to export raw materials and industrial products for foreign exchange; these activities often conflict with longer-term ecological considerations.

Deforestation, for example, has several causes. One is the expanding population of nomadic cultivators, who often systematically cull the wood around their base camps or villages. Another is cutting for firewood—the main source of energy for roughly a fourth of humankind. Other causes are commercial logging for export to rich nations and clearance for cattle-grazing. The world's forests are presently disappearing at an estimated rate of 11 to 18 million hectares a year. The rate of tree plantation in the tropics amounts to less than one-tenth of the rate of deforestation. It has been calculated that up to three billion people could live in areas short of fuelwood by 2000.

If tropical forests continue to be cleared at the current rate, an estimated 10 to 20 percent of the earth's plant and animal life will be lost by the year 2000. One can only speculate as to the full implications for the planet's gene bank, the climate, the production of oxygen, and so on.

Job Outlook

Unemployment and under-employment are already estimated to be running at 40-50 percent in poor nations. The International Labor Organization (ILO) projects an increase of 1.4 billion workers in the developing regions between 1985 and 2025. Some 30 years ago the migration of millions of unemployed people from the countryside to the cities began on a massive scale. If developing countries double their population every 25 to 35 years, their major cities will often do so in 10 to 15 years, some 60 percent of that growth being due to natural increase.

A quarter of the world's families live in makeshift shelters. Fully half of the Third World's urban dwellers live in shanty towns which double in population every seven to ten years.

A report just published by the World Health Organization (WHO) and United Nations Environment Program (UNEP) has been widely quoted as stating that the air breathed by many of the world's city-dwellers is not fit for humans. Urbanization and high birth rates have also overtaxed water supplies and sewage systems. What will the situation look like in 2025 when the world will have some 135 cities with populations of over four million, most of them in developing countries?

Women Bear the Brunt

In all developing regions, lowered rates of population increase would free resources to improve the quantity and quality of education and reduce female illiteracy substantially. Indications are that the number of female illiterates will increase much faster than the number of male illiterates. In 1985, the female illiteracy rate, at 49 percent of adult women, was almost twice the male rate of 28 percent.

These percentages are not unrelated to the rapid population increase, for which women have borne the heaviest costs, both through the extra work load and the health risks connected with pregnancies and births that are too many, too frequent, too early and too late. Between 35 and 50 million abortions are thought to be carried out annually on women desperate not to go through with their latest pregnancy. Some half a million women die every year from conditions arising from pregnancy or child birth. The morbidity toll is unknown. It has been estimated that extended family planning services could save 200,000 women each year. It would also help reduce infant mortality.

But family planning on its own will not be enough. In the words of the United Nations Fund for Population Activities (UNFPA), "women in most developing countries still derive their status in their community from their positions as wives and mothers. An important contribution of lower fertility will be a change in the way women derive their status. Contributing to a change are the legal right to own and inherit property, the right to vote, the right to choice in marriage and divorce, education, acknowledged life options other than childbearing—and, access to family planning information and services. These are desirable changes in their own right, regardless of their impact on fertility.

37

5   DEBATING POPULATION GROWTH

LIFE IS GETTING BETTER

Julian L. Simon

Julian Simon teaches business administration at the University of Maryland and has published several books on population including The Ultimate Resource *and* Population Matters.

Points to Consider:

1. Why are people the "ultimate resource"?

2. How has population growth improved our lives?

3. What is the relationship between population growth and the supply of resources? Explain.

4. How do food prices relate to population growth?

Julian L. Simon, "Too Few People? Too Many Trees?", **Crisis**, February 1991. Reprinted by permission of **Crisis** Magazine, 1511 K Street NW., Suite 525, Washington, D.C. 20005.

There is only one important resource which has shown a trend of increasing scarcity rather than increasing abundance. That resource is the most important of all—human beings.

Once again we are hearing the plaintive laments: too many people, too little food, too few trees. If the world could just learn to control its population, it is said, the environment would be safer from grubby human paws, and food could then be distributed or redistributed so that everyone could eat well and be happy.

This rhetoric goes on and on. We hear that "world peace is threatened by the plundering of natural resources and by a progressive decline in the quality of life." Also of "the existence, especially in the southern hemisphere, of a demographic problem which creates difficulties for development." And of "limits of available resources" and of "the need to respect the integrity and cycles of nature. . .an ecological concern."

The key question before us is whether more people are beneficial or detrimental with respect to human progress. The most important and amazing demographic fact—the most important human achievement in history, in my view—is the decrease in the world's death rate. It took thousands of years to increase life expectancy at birth from just over 20 years to the high 20s. Yet in just the last two centuries, life expectancy at birth in the advanced countries jumped from less than 30 years to roughly 75 years.

Ultimate Resource

Then, since World War II, life expectancy in the poor countries has leaped upwards—by perhaps 15 or even 20 years since the 1950s—because of advances in agriculture, sanitation, and medicine. Is this not an astounding triumph for humankind? This decrease in the death rate is the cause of there being a larger world population now than in former times.

One would expect lovers of humankind to jump with joy at this triumph of mind and heart over the raw forces of nature. Instead, many lament that there are so many people alive to enjoy the gift of life. And it is this worry—a misplaced concern, as we shall see—that leads them to approve inhumane programs of coercion and denial of personal liberty in one of the most precious choices a family can make: the number of children the couple wishes to bear and raise.

Throughout history, adequacy of supplies of natural resources has always been a source of concern that has led to calls for population control. Yet the data clearly show that natural resource scarcity, as measured by the economically meaningful indicator of price, has been decreasing rather than increasing in the long run for all raw materials, with only temporary exceptions from time to time.

Food is an especially important resource. A typical doomsaying forecast came from a key document of the environmentalist movement, the *Global 2000 Report to President Carter*: "Real prices for food are expected to double" by the year 2000, it said. But the evidence is particularly strong that food prices are on a downward trend despite rising population. The long-run prices of food relative to wages, and even relative to consumer products, is down due to increased productivity.

Famine deaths due to insufficient food supply have decreased during the past century even in absolute terms, let alone relative to population, a matter which pertains particularly to the poor countries. Per-person food consumption is up over the last 30 years, and there are no data showing that the bottom of the income scale is faring worse, or even has failed to share in the general nutritional improvement, as the average has improved.

There is only one important resource which has shown a trend of increasing scarcity rather than increasing abundance. That resource is the most important of all—human beings. Yes, there are more people on earth now than ever before. But if we measure the scarcity of people the same way that we measure the scarcity of other economic goods—by how much we must pay to obtain their services—we see that wages and salaries have been going up all over the world, in poor countries as well as in rich countries. This increase in the price of peoples' services is a clear indication that people are becoming more scarce economically, even though there are more of us.

A Better Life

The evidence with respect to air indicates that pollutants have been declining, especially the most dangerous type of pollutant, particulates (the dirty black stuff thrown into the air from chimneys, the cause of the old London fogs and increased death rates). With respect to water, the proportion of monitored sites in the U.S. having water of good drinkability has increased since the data began in 1961.

To sum up the statistical history, there now are more people on earth than ever before, and also better material conditions of life than ever before. A reasonable first-order hypothesis, then, is that a larger population leads to a better life rather than to a poorer life.

More people, and increased income, cause problems in the short-run. These problems present opportunities and prompt the search for solutions. In a free society, solutions are eventually found, and in the long-run the new developments leave us better off than if the problems had not arisen.

Yes, more consumers means less of the fixed available stock of goods to be divided among more people. And more workers laboring with the same fixed current stock of capital means that there will be less output per worker. The latter effect, known as "the law of diminishing returns," is the essence of Malthus' theory as he first set it out.

But if the resources with which people work are not fixed over the period being analyzed, then the Malthusian logic of diminishing returns does not apply. And the plain fact is that, given some time to adjust to shortages, the resource base does not remain fixed. People create more resources of all kinds.

The Long View

When we take a long-run view, the picture is different, and considerably more complex, than the simple short-run view of more people implying lower average income. In the very long-run, more people almost surely imply more available resources and a higher income for everyone.

At the heart of a free, market-directed economic system, according to Friedrich Hayek, are two general institutions: privateness of property, and the family. They are both necessary for economic development. An unfree, centrally-directed socialist system will necessarily prevent the free existence of these two institutions. It is no wonder that the Church's traditional teachings come into conflict with those of communist regimes.

Twenty or even ten years ago these ideas about population growth were so far out of the mainstream of scientific discussion that a person might prudently have continued to be skeptical even if the arguments and data made sense in themselves. But in the last few years there has been a radical shift in the views on these matters held by economic demographers as well as by official institutions.

The official U.S. National Research Council of the National Academy of Sciences issued a major report in 1971 that said population growth prevents economic growth. But in 1986 the

41

National Academy of Sciences issued another major report that almost completely reversed the 1971 report. For example, it now says that "the scarcity of exhaustible resources is at most a minor constraint on economic growth in the near to intermediate term. On balance, then, we find that concern about the impact of rapid population growth on resource exhaustion has often been exaggerated."

People Power

The Pope recognized the horror of the actions to which some countries such as China have resorted due to the belief in "overpopulation" which he shares, and he properly denounces those actions. "It is very alarming to see governments in many countries launching systematic campaigns against birth." If the Church will come to recognize what demographic-economic science has arrived at during the past few years—that contrary to conventional belief, more births are not economically detrimental in the long-run, and that the problem of China is not her population but rather her socialistic system that prevents development—the Church can then bring its moral position into consonance with its assumptions and aspirations.

Adding more people causes short-run problems, but people are also the means to solve these problems. The main fuel to speed the world's progress is our stock of knowledge, and the brake is our lack of imagination. The ultimate resource is people—skilled, spirited, and hopeful people—who will exert their will and imagination for their own benefit as well as in a spirit of

42

faith and social concern, and so inevitably they will benefit not only themselves but the poor and the rest of us as well.

6 DEBATING POPULATION GROWTH

POPULATION GROWTH CAUSES POVERTY

Don Hinrichsen

Don Hinrichsen is a contributing editor of The Amicus Journal.

Points to Consider:

1. Who is the "global underclass"? Why?

2. How is the environment affected by population growth?

3. Describe the "population transition".

4. How is poverty related to rapid population growth?

5. What is meant by the term "decisive decade"?

High population growth rates aggravate poverty and impede economic development.

Numbers may be numbing, but the arithmetic of population growth and the urban explosion can no longer be ignored. There is no doubt that the human ark is bulging at the seams. Every day we share the earth and its resources with 250,000 more people than the day before. Every year there are another 90 million mouths to feed. That is the equivalent of adding a city the size of Philadelphia to the world population every week; a Los Angeles every two weeks; a Mexico every year; and a United States and Canada every three years.

Though fertility rates are dropping, the sheer momentum of population growth ensures that at least another three billion people will be crowded onto the planet between now and the year 2025. At current growth rates, one billion people are added to the ark every eleven years.

Global Underclass

If these trends are not reversed or at least slowed down, we could be facing a global population of close to 14 billion by the year 2100. But the problem is not population growth *per se.* "The problem is that over 90 percent of the people being born now live in the developing world, those countries least able to cope with the resource and environmental consequences of burgeoning populations," points out Alex Marshall, deputy director of information at the United Nations Population Fund. A simple comparison shows the dichotomy. Between now and the turn of the century, the population of industrialized countries will grow by only 56 million, or 5.2 percent, while that of the Third World will balloon to over 900 million, a staggering 25 percent increase.

Unfortunately, many of the people born over the course of the next few decades in the Third World will find themselves at the bottom of the heap, locked into grinding poverty with little hope of escape. The number of households living in what writer Erik Eckholm calls the "global underclass" is expected to reach nearly one billion by the year 2000, more than double the number of absolute poor recorded in 1975.

Environmental Pressures

Much of the damage inflicted on the developing world's environment comes from the bottom billion poorest people,

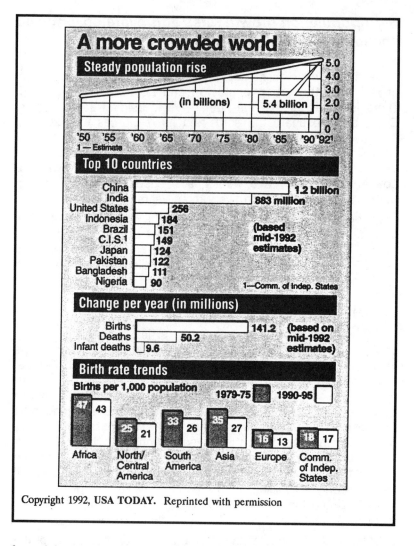

A more crowded world

Steady population rise

(in billions)

5.4 billion

5.0
4.0
3.0
2.0
1.0
0

'50 '55 '60 '65 '70 '75 '80 '85 '90 '92¹

1 — Estimate

Top 10 countries

China	1.2 billion
India	883 million
United States	256
Indonesia	184
Brazil	151
C.I.S.¹	149
Japan	124
Pakistan	122
Bangladesh	111
Nigeria	90

(based mid-1992 estimates)

1—Comm. of Indep. States

Change per year (in millions)

Births	141.2
Deaths	50.2
Infant deaths	9.6

(based on mid-1992 estimates)

Birth rate trends

Births per 1,000 population   ▨ 1979-75   ☐ 1990-95

Africa	North/Central America	South America	Asia	Europe	Comm. of Indep. States
47 / 43	25 / 21	33 / 26	35 / 27	16 / 13	18 / 17

forced by poverty and sheer weight of numbers to over-exploit limited resources. But the top billion richest also contribute their share to the destruction through "indirect" consumer preferences. The Japanese wood chip industry in Indonesia, for example, clears more mangrove trees than poor fisherfolk who cut them down to build fish and shrimp ponds. Much of the wood hauled out of tropical forests ends up as furniture, paneling, and veneer in rich world homes.

Globally, we are losing a minimum of 15 million acres of prime agricultural land to over-use and mismanagement every year. Desertification is threatening about one-third of the world's land surface, or 16 million square miles. Tropical rain forests, repositories of immense biological wealth, are being destroyed at the rate of 25 million acres a year, an area roughly the size of Austria. Through a combination of ignorance, greed, and neglect, we may be condemning several million species of plants and animals to the awful finality of extinction by the turn of the century. To complicate matters, there are holes in our ozone shield, and climate change on a global scale threatens to alter rainfall patterns and raise sea levels.

Population Transition

Although resource and environmental issues affect every country, runaway population growth is almost exclusively a developing world problem. The "population transition" has been made in the highly developed countries of Europe, Asia, and North America. Populations in Europe and North America, for example, have stabilized and are growing on average by only one to two percent a year.

Much of the Third World, however, has yet to make this critical transition—from rapid population growth rates to sustainable ones. In many developing countries, particularly in Africa and the Middle East, growth rates hover around three percent a year, doubling their populations every twenty-three years.

One of the reasons for continued high population growth rates is that the average woman in Africa and the Middle East bears between six and eight children during her reproductive years. Children are seen as assets, not liabilities. Large families are culturally acceptable and socially desirable. In some countries, like Senegal, nine children per woman is the norm. Compare this against a global average of slightly more than four children per woman; in industrialized countries it is only two.

Poverty

High population growth rates aggravate poverty and impede economic development. As human numbers continue to outpace resources, Third World countries cannot cope with the consequences. The results are only too evident: mounting unemployment; spreading slums and squatter settlements; lack of access to clean water and sanitation facilities; not enough school rooms; too few doctors, nurses, teachers, and other skilled professionals; and no (or very limited) access to family planning services. Poverty deepens. More people are pushed to the edge of survival.

Although growth rates in Asia and Latin America are beginning to slow down as population programs and family planning services take root, the crisis is far from over. In the crowded countries of China, India, Bangladesh, Indonesia and the Philippines, human numbers are already bumping into resources limitations. Consider the Philippines. Most poor Filipinos were better off a decade ago than they are today. Nearly half of the entire population—about 29 million—live at or below the poverty line. Pressure on the country's coastlines is so intense that fish stocks have plummeted in many areas.

Getting out of poverty and indebtedness is made more difficult by the youthfulness of Third World populations. According to the United Nations Population Fund, in 1985 around 37 percent of the total population in the developing world—1.3 billion—were children below the age of fifteen. In Africa, where fertility has remained markedly high, children make up nearly 50 percent of the population. This many dependents puts added strain on creaky economies.

But in the final analysis, it is lack of access to family planning and health services that really makes a big difference in individual family size. The World Fertility Survey, carried out in forty-one developing countries between 1972 and 1984, revealed a striking unmet need for contraception and family planning. If all women who said they wanted no more children were able to stop childbearing, the number of births would be reduced by 27 percent in Africa, 33 percent in Asia, and 35 percent in Latin America. These figures imply a cruelly inadequate supply of contraception to women who want it, and a growing need for family planning services.

Decade For Action

Former West German Chancellor Willy Brandt, in a keynote

48

address to the International Forum on Population in th
Twenty-first Century held in Amsterdam in 1989, referred to
decade of the 1980s as "a lost decade for developme.
cooperation". In assessing the failures of the past, Brandt
suggested that the role played by the multilateral agencies of the
United Nations and other international organizations be
strengthened by joining forces to address the critical
developmental, population, and environmental issues facing
Africa, Latin America, and Asia. "We need capable international
and regional organizations for a broad surveillance of the
performance of national governments, regardless of their power
status," Brandt told the assembled delegates from over eighty
countries. "We probably need something like a security council
for the global environment and population matters."

A few years ago, talk like this would have drawn yawns from
policymakers from north and south alike. No longer. If the
indecisive 1980s were the "lost decade", the 1990s promise to
be the decade for decision and action.

"What we do over the course of the next decade will
determine the future of our planet," insists Nafis Sadik, executive
director of the United Nations Population Fund (UNFPA) in New
York. "Governments have started to recognize this. They have
started to see that these great increases in population are
reducing their ability to respond effectively to the crisis of
resources."

Brandt and Sadik, among a chorus of others, consider the
next ten years to be absolutely critical—a decade during which
the global community must confront the challenges of population
growth and distribution, urbanization, resource use, and
environmental deterioration on a broad scale. Decisions
postponed and actions not taken during this period will have
devastating consequences for the generations of the twenty-first
century.

Sadik, a former medical doctor from Pakistan, who has been
with UNFPA for nearly twenty years, is convinced that nothing
short of integrated planning on both a national and international
level will get effective results in time to make a difference. "We
(the UN) need to begin strategic, integrated planning of our own
programs, but governments must be encouraged to do the
same," she affirms.

POVERTY CAUSES
POPULATION GROWTH

Wangari Maathi

Professor Wangari Maathi is a member of the Greenbelt Movement, a project founded by the National Council for the Women of Kenya.

Points to Consider

1. How does poverty cause population growth?

2. Why do rights of women have a relationship to population?

3. How is the relationship between God and poor people described?

4. Why is traditional farming better than cash crop agriculture?

Excerpted from testimony by Professor Wangari Maathi before the House Committee on Science, Space and Technology, February 28, 1989.

The more affluent are the ones who are concerned about the rapid increase in population.

Food production in Africa has fallen repeatedly in the recent past, and they blame the poor for it. In some areas, famine is a recurrent phenomenon. Africans are constantly fighting hunger, and have been forced to import food. Among the leading causes of poor crop yield is over-exploitation of land and loss of topsoil. Yet farmers have no choice but to continue to grow crops on highly impoverished soils.

Cash Crops and Traditional Farming

Chemical fertilizers, pesticides, new seed varieties and huge irrigation schemes are some of the solutions being offered to African farmers. These solutions will not work. They won't work because fertilizers and pesticides cost too much in foreign currency to be sustained.

Assuming that the current world order will not change overnight, African farmers have but one choice — work with Nature to produce as much food as possible. As part of this, they should be reminded that there is wisdom in traditional farming practices.

The increasing amount of land used for cash crops is another factor that keeps Africa from producing enough food. In Central Kenya, for example, malnutrition is partly due to the fact that cash crops are replacing food crops.

This is not to say that cash crops should be abandoned. Far from it. But considering the current world economic order, it is quite possible that people could over-exploit their resources in order to produce raw materials for export, only to earn too little to meet even their basic needs like food. People should be encouraged to grow their own food as much as possible.

Food Production

Another reason for inadequate food production is the low priority given to agriculture. Food production in Africa is a responsibility relegated to small farmers — mostly women — who are not a priority for Africans. It is part of the "colonial heritage" that our universities and institutes are still producing white collar, laboratory-bound or office and extension workers.

A rural survey in Kenya showed that "research has failed to focus on food crops of women's agricultural efforts." The same report notes that "the lower level of education attainment of rural

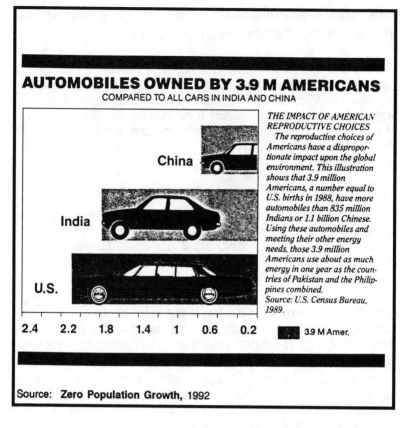

AUTOMOBILES OWNED BY 3.9 M AMERICANS
COMPARED TO ALL CARS IN INDIA AND CHINA

China

India

U.S.

| 2.4 | 2.2 | 1.8 | 1.4 | 1 | 0.6 | 0.2 | | 3.9 M Amer. |

THE IMPACT OF AMERICAN REPRODUCTIVE CHOICES
The reproductive choices of Americans have a disproportionate impact upon the global environment. This illustration shows that 3.9 million Americans, a number equal to U.S. births in 1988, have more automobiles than 835 million Indians or 1.1 billion Chinese. Using these automobiles and meeting their other energy needs, those 3.9 million Americans use about as much energy in one year as the countries of Pakistan and the Philippines combined.
Source: U.S. Census Bureau, 1989.

Source: **Zero Population Growth,** 1992

women partly accounts for the low female participation rates in activities other than farming." Thus, farming (other than farming of cash crops) is a job relegated to the uneducated—those who are unemployable as white-collar workers. These are mostly rural women.

Agriculture for food production must become a priority for Africa if famine is to end. It has to become economically attractive to have well-trained farmers. Africans need to appreciate that while they are dying of hunger, some countries have too much food. And if they cannot find the funds to import this food, the only alternative to starvation is for Africans to produce their own food.

Food Security

Food security can become a reality for Africa if Africans make agriculture a priority. Root crops and drought-resistant crops have always been Africa's hope for hard times. Coupled with improved food processing and storage facilities, they could ease the burden of famine. But these crops are ignored by Africa's elite, and it is these people who sit in the Ministries of Agriculture and Economic Planning and make decisions.

Small farmers, particularly women farmers, should be supported if food production is to increase in Africa. Unfortunately, these are the farmers that are the most minimized. They are the farmers that are the most ignored and considered peripheral in national economics. And they have neither the political power nor the economic power needed to demand better compensation for their labor or to prevent subsidized food imports.

Ironically, while they have been pushed to the periphery of the economy, they are central to food production. This must change if famine is to end. We must empower the small farmers. Then, perhaps, agriculture in Africa will attract educated, dedicated and resourceful Africans who will be willing to produce enough food to feed Africans.

If not, African elites will have to spend more foreign exchange purchasing arms to protect themselves and their interests. For when citizens become poor and hungry, they become politically unstable and difficult to govern. The enemy, then, rises from within, not from across borders. If current trends continue, political instabilities and military *coups d'etat* can only increase.

It is important to understand the population issue and how it inter-relates with under-development, poverty and environmental degradation. At four percent and rising, Kenya's population growth is among the highest in the world. It is a trend that can be seen throughout Africa. However, the more affluent are the ones who are concerned about the rapid increase in population. And they blame the poor for it. But why are there so many people?

Some of the world's poverty is caused by injustices created by the current world economic order. To call upon the poor to improve their situation within the current economic order is unrealistic. Hence the call for a new economic order, especially by governments of the less industrialized world.

Rapid population growth has also to do with the rights of women. Some communities oppose any efforts by women to acquire basic human rights and freedom regarding population issues. They deny women the rights of self-determination and self-fulfillment. As long as this prevails, it will be difficult to control the population growth and realize sustainable development. Indeed, we will be even more entangled in vicious circles which cause regression, instability and even more widespread poverty.

This is because suppressed, poverty-stricken and hungry people do not plan their families and they are not concerned with environmental conservation, even though they are the first victims of environmental degradation. They do not take their destiny into their own hands.

Hope in God

Instead, they place all their hope in God. They seem to pray, "Since you are God, work miracles so that I may survive. Make it possible for me to satisfy my basic needs." They (the people) are not aware that they have not used all the wonderful talents and resources they already have. They are asking God to be a magician, a miracle worker.

Many Africans have abandoned their traditional concept of God and embraced a new and foreign concept. Their cultures, traditions, values and virtues have been deliberately eroded and debased under the pretense that they are satanic and will keep them from God in Heaven.

And it is from this new power that they expect magic. For if calamities like poverty, hunger and drought are perceived as natural and, therefore, acts of God, Africans have every reason to doubt the power of their traditional God and expect miracles from the new (European) God who seems to protect Europeans from such calamities.

But there is growing evidence (even among the Africans) that these calamities are not acts of God but of humans. If that is so, Africans have to examine where they, rather than God, went wrong. Having more children than one can take care of, being poor, preventing the earth from bearing fruit—these and other adversities should not be blamed on God. They are the acts of men and women. And it is up to us to turn things around with or without the blessing of our leaders.

Time has shown that those who do not work with Mother Earth are punished or eliminated by Her. She blesses us only if we are wise and work with Her, if we learn to be Her custodians and to appreciate how all life forms on this planet earth are related.

U.S. POPULATION GROWTH:
Points and Counterpoints

Don Feder
vs.
Zero Population Growth

Don Feder is a nationaly syndicated columnist. He wrote the following article for Creators Syndicate, Inc. *The comments by* Zero Population Growth *were excerpted from a ZPG public position paper.*

Points to Consider

1. How many American births result from unintended pregnancy?

2. What evidence is cited to support the idea of a problem of under-population in the U.S.?

3. What evidence is cited to support the idea of a problem of over-population in the U.S.?

4. Do you agree with the point or the counterpoint? Why?

Zero Population Growth public position paper dated February, 1992, and Don Feder, "Big families are socially responsible", **Conservative Chronicle**, November 6, 1991, copyright **Boston Herald.** By permission of Don Feder and **Creators Syndicate.**

THE POINT — Don Feder

It was "the most socially responsible thing I've done in a long time," trilled *Washington Monthly* contributing editor Scott Shuger of his vasectomy. A paladin of population control, Shuger put his reproductive organs on the line, and now preens for our approval.

"An alarming 40 percent of births in this country result from unintended pregnancy," Shyger breathlessly informs us. Horror, imagine — life happening spontaneously! (Nature can be so messy.) The fault lies with men, he confesses in a spasm of new-mannish gender guilt. We are "birth control wimps".

Based on his personal experience, Shuger is so high on cut, cut — snip, snip that he urges a campaign on the scale of Desert Storm to persuade men that sterile-is-beautiful, including "aggressive out-reach" and more bucks for woefully underfunded family planning programs. After all, sex education and contraceptive expenditures only increased twentyfold (from $l3.5 million to $279 million) between 1969 and 1979.

The piece ends in an orgy of new male-bonding, as Shuger describes his cheerful banter with the medics who fixed him. Ah, the joys of '90s manhood.

Unstated Premises

There are a number of unstated premises here, to which the author alludes with his self-congratulatory pat on the social conscience: that America is in imminent danger of being buried under the debris from a detonating population bomb, that too many people will capsize spaceship earth, that "unwanted" children are an awful burden.

Before pushing the panic button, it's important to understand what is meant by an "unplanned pregnancy". According to the population controllers, unless a child is desired by both partners at the point of conception (never-mind how they feel later), it's an unplanned pregnancy, hence a serious social concern.

Did Mr. and Mrs. Washington "plan" their fifth child, the one who grew up to be our first president? In a culture obsessed with arranging every detail of existence (education, career, retirement, even leisure pursuits), the unintended is ominous.

America's demographic problem in the next century won't be a population deluge but a birth dearth. Our birth rate has hovered just below replacement level for the past two decades, plunging from 3.77 children per woman in 1957 to 2.0 today.

The nation's birthrate is actually lower now than in 1944, when 7,447,000 young men were serving overseas.

Evidence of the Empty Cradle

Evidence of the empty cradle crisis may be seen in the graying of our nation, the schools transformed into senior housing, the baby clothes manufacturers scaling back their operations while pharmaceutical firms, whose profits rest with seniors, enjoy unprecedented boom.

As Thomas Fleming notes in *Chronicles*, the population control visionaries "refuse to distinguish between the American middle class and the beggars of Calcutta." The former fire an industrial engine which produces a quarter of the world's manufactured goods.

Regrettably, the people least likely to heed Shuger's call to social responsibility are residents of Third World ant heaps and the 17-year-old unwed mother with her teeming welfare brood, not to mention her bevy of unemployed boyfriends. Those most susceptible to the call to class suicide, through guilt or misperceived self-interest, are the nice suburban couple. The children they never had might have grown up to write a symphony, develop a revolutionary manufacturing process or find a cure for daytime television.

An industrial civilization can't be maintained without people. The population rise of the modern era paved the way for the Industrial Revolution of the late 18th and early 19th centuries. Because our parents and grandparents chose to have large families, we can enjoy the amenities of modern America, giving us the opportunity to neglect our procreative duties for career advancement, two-paycheck families and a dazzling array of pleasures.

But what will come after us? How will today's demographic drought support a comparable living standard for future generations? If you have the means to support them, and the values to raise them well, having a large family is the most socially responsible thing you can do.

Beyond all of this, procreation is a celebration of life. To voluntarily relinquish the ability to create life makes a profound statement of regard for the same. It also bespeaks a loss of faith, an insistence that we, and not our Maker, know best when it comes to determining family size. How well the psalmist put it "Behold, children are a gift of the Lord; The fruit of the womb is a reward. Like arrows in the hands of a warrior, so are the children of one's youth." (Psalm 127:3-5)

In a way it's fitting that an increasingly sterile culture of plastic values and throw-away relationships would embrace contraception with almost religious fervor.

THE COUNTERPOINT — Zero Population Growth

Right now, we are heading on a collision course toward a population crisis—not only in distant developing countries of Africa and Latin America, but right here in the United States. If population growth continues at its present rate, we will have squeezed—through births, legal and illegal immigration—another 40 million people inside U.S. boundaries by the year 2000. Already, our country is adding the population equivalent of four Washington, D.C.s every year, another New Jersey every three years, another California every twelve. Those are staggering figures—with far-reaching implications for you and every concerned American.

No matter how distracted we may be by the number of problems now facing us, one issue remains so fundamental that most can agree on its urgency: overpopulation, the crowding of our cities underlies all other problems. You see, unless steps are taken now to address population growth in this country and abroad, census statistics will continue to swell, with mind-boggling consequences affecting every aspect of life as we know it.

Already, around the world, you can see with frightening clarity the damage caused by overpopulation: globally, over one billion people suffer from malnutrition, with 14 million children under the age of five dying each year! Hunger and overpopulation are inextricably linked in places like Africa, where devastating drought—combined with the fastest population growth in all of human history—has led to widespread famine. In Mexico City, now the world's most populous city, 40% of its 22 million inhabitants are forced to live in slums. And both Mexico and Central America, already facing unemployment rates as high as 50 percent, can expect a tripling of their labor force in less than 50 years!

Even though Americans make up only five percent of world population, we consume 11 times the world's average in energy, six times the steel, and four times the grain. Because of such heavy consumption of resources, even small population increases here can adversely affect countries around the world.

But the surprising reality—the one most Americans don't know about or choose to ignore—is that other, equally ominous danger signals of overpopulation exist right here in our own backyard:

- In Los Angeles and Phoenix, where air pollution abounds and water supplies are dangerously scarce;
- In the Florida Everglades, where human competition for water and habitat has evicted or destroyed a disturbing number of native wildlife species, including the endangered Florida panther and peregrine falcon;
- And on the Chesapeake Bay, where overdevelopment contaminates water quality and degrades shoreline ecology.

Wherever you live, you may already be victim to some of the early warning signs: Drinking water poisoned by excessive and poorly processed toxic wastes. Vital topsoil and farmland lost to development of shopping centers, highways, subdivisions — at the alarming pace of one million acres each year!

And the rapid dwindling of American wildlife — including the grizzly bear, California condor, sea otter. (In fact, if population demands necessitate continued cutting of the planet's tropical forests, at least one-fourth of all wildlife species could disappear within the next 50 years!)

With over a one percent annual growth rate, the United States is already adding well over two million people yearly - making us the world's fourth most populous nation. ANY large population increase here can put a serious strain on our nation's health facilities and schools — and multiply already troubling unemployment figures. At no time have I been more concerned about the population crisis — in America and the rest of the world than I am right now.

With the number of women of child-bearing age at an all time high, an increase in immigration and an actively hostile right-wing opposition to population planning efforts, the United States today is one of the fastest-growing of all industrialized nations. NOTHING is more urgent than focusing national attention on the problems such runaway population growth can bring.

Since our inception in 1968, Zero Population Growth has worked to educate and motivate people to meet the global population challenge and to understand the impact of our consumption, lifestyles and technology on the Earth.

We believe that each individual, each couple should have the means and knowledge to decide freely, responsibly and without coercion whether and when to have a family. And we want to see our government establish a population policy that

60

encourages voluntary family planning and sets the goal of stopping population growth in the U.S. and worldwide.

EXAMINING COUNTERPOINTS

This activity may be used as an individualized study guide for students in libraries and resource centers or as a discussion catalyst in small group and classroom discussions.

The Point

Overpopulation poses a serious threat to Western nations and the whole planet. While the world population has grown from three billion in 1960 to over five billion today, the U.S. has been adding some two million people to its population each year and at current rates will grow from over 250 million now to over 400 million by 2050.

At these rates, the industrialized nations can expect continued strain on an already deteriorating environment and quality of life. The U.S. alone loses one million acres of topsoil each year to development and may lose up to one-fourth of its wildlife in the next 50 years. Increased population in the West will continue to demand more of the world's precious resources, making matters worse for the developing nations.

We must limit our own growth to an average of under two children per family and limit immigration which now comprises 40 percent of the annual U.S. increase. Our priorities must also include wiser use of resources in order to feed today's current population.

The Counterpoint

With fertility rates declining, the Western industrialized nations are facing a serious population shortage. We are simply not producing enough children to maintain a stable population. Today the U.S. has its lowest fertility rate since the Great Depression of the 1930s. The overpopulation "bomb" has turned out to be a bomb of "fear". Current figures show that while the "baby-boomers" in America averaged 2.4 children per family, their kids are projected to average only 1.6, well under the 2.1 figure needed to reproduce ourselves.

Who will pay future Medicaid, Social Security and pension tabs? Today's young people will need to support more and more elderly in the years ahead. Slower growth rates will decrease our labor markets, our standard of living and our relative power in global affairs as developing nations surge ahead.

The U.S. and other Western nations must strive to maintain a level of at least two children per family, as most citizens in Europe and America are against any increased immigration. Government tax incentives for larger families would be one way to help insure a stable population and secure future.

Guidelines

Social issues are usually complex, but often problems become oversimplified in political debates and discussion. Usually a polarized version of social conflict does not adequately represent the diversity of views that surround social conflicts.

1. Examine the counterpoints above. Then write down possible interpretations of this issue other than the two arguments stated in the counterpoints above.

2. How do the figures cited in each opinion support that position?

3. Do the statistics used in the point necessarily refute those in the counterpoint?

4. Do any of the authors in Chapter Two agree with either of the counterpoints? If so, which one(s)?

CHAPTER 3

POPULATION AND THE ENVIRONMENT

POPULATION AND THE
ENVIRONMENT

POPULATION GROWTH HARMS
THE ENVIRONMENT

Werner Fornos

*Werner Fornos is director of the Population Institute and has also worked
on family planning programs in many Third World nations.*

Points to Consider:

1. What are the ecological costs of population growth?

2. How does urbanization affect the environment?

3. Why are demographics important?

4. What must be done to avoid environmental "armageddon"?

Werner Fornos, "Gaining People, Losing Ground", **The Humanist**, May/June 1990.

The short-sighted policies of the present are dangerously narrowing our options for avoiding environmental armageddon.

Ignoring the problem of rapid population growth in the developing world could be the ultimate global blunder—one from which there may be no recovery. The short-sighted policies of the present are dangerously narrowing our options for avoiding environmental armageddon.

As the risk of thermo-nuclear war between the superpowers finally shows substantial signs of fading, at least some portion of the funds used in the arms race for the past forty years can now be redirected to the issues that may determine our very survival. Among the priority uses for this peace dividend must be the assistance required from the industrialized world so that developing nations may be able to cope with the problem of too many people and too few resources—a problem that lies at the root of, or at least exacerbates, the poverty and deprivation in Third World countries.

Ravages of Pollution

During this week alone, another 1.7 million people will be added to the world. Another 750,000 acres of Brazilian rain forest will be destroyed. Pollution of developing world waterways and the buildup of greenhouse gases will have accelerated just a little from the week before. The dangers inherent in a world population outgrowing its environmental resources demand a new commitment to reshaping our future. We in the industrialized world—especially the United States—need dynamic political change. We must abandon our current crisis-oriented government philosophy and replace it with one that looks to the decades to come—not just to the next election.

Pollution, once thought to be primarily a problem of the industrialized world, is today a crisis for the developing world. To a greater or lesser degree, industrialized nations are implementing efforts to control or mitigate the pollution associated with factories and cities. However, the Third World countries pressing hard for rapid development cannot afford the often costly technology required to minimize the resulting pollution. We are entering the transnational decade. Pollution does not respect national boundaries. Relying upon wood as the basic fuel—as 70 percent of Third World families do—contributes to the carbon dioxide buildup. So does burning low-grade coal, which in 1989 led to the destruction of the salmon crop in

Two Economic Models

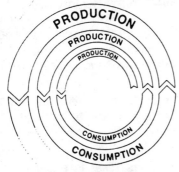

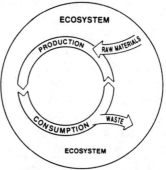

Standard Economics

Standard economics considers ever-growing cycles of production and consumption but does not consider the role of the supporting ecosystem. Such a view can encourage an economy which can ultimately strain the surrounding environment.

Steady-State Economics

Steady-state economics considers cycles of production and consumption which take the surrounding ecosystem into account and try to achieve a state of equilibrium with it.

Source: **Zero Population Growth,** 1992

Norway by acid rain from Great Britain.

Urbanization

A second danger which must be recognized is the swift urbanization of the poorer nations. By the end of this century, nineteen of the world's twenty-one largest metropolitan areas will be located in developing countries. Densely crowded slums, snarled traffic, faulty or nonexistent sewage and waste disposal systems, and sprawling, inefficient industrial operations will contribute to polluted, smog-ridden cities.

Scientists have further concluded that the giant "hole" in the ozone layer discovered over the south pole is not the result of natural causes, as first suspected, but, rather, of humankind's pollution of the atmosphere. Chlorofluorocarbons (CFCs), the chief culprit in the depletion of the ozone layer, are a common element found in refrigerators, air conditioners, and many industrial solvents. It takes one molecule of CFC fifteen years to reach the stratosphere, some seventeen to twenty-five miles above us. This means the damage that has now resulted in international concern was created in 1975. Since then, our reliance upon these gases has increased by 100 percent. We really do not know how much damage we have caused to the atmosphere.

Meanwhile, the world's population of 5.3 billion is expected to reach six billion by the middle of this decade, and, at the present rate, it will double within forty years.

The worst news is that in this generation, three billion young people will enter their reproductive years. That is equal to the entire world population in 1960. How well these young people are able to implement the basic human right of having only those children they truly want, can care for and love, will mean the difference between a twenty-first century in which we are headed for a better quality of life, or environmental armageddon.

Demographics

Hidden in these statistics is the fact that we are living in a demographically divided world. This past year, the world population grew by 92 million—the largest annual increase ever recorded. Over 90 percent of that growth occurred in the developing world, where economies are stagnating and societies are torn by civil strife, social unrest, and brutal poverty.

Not all is bad news. In some thirty countries where the political will exists to do something about the problem, where motivation for smaller families is part of the culture, and where the education and means for controlling one's fertility are readily available, the growth rates and fertility rates are decreasing. Indonesia, China, Thailand, South Korea, Mexico, Brazil, Zimbabwe, and Tunisia are among these countries. But in ninety other nations, despite their desire to escape the demographic trap they are caught in, the populations will have doubled in thirty years or less.

The worst situation exists in Africa, where growth rates are still increasing and where an average of six to eight children per woman is the norm. Moreover, there are cultural and social barriers to bringing down fertility. The old arguments of boys carrying on the family tradition and children providing for their parents' old-age security still abound, but some 500 million women responding to a world fertility survey said that they do not want more children. However, most of them lack the education and the means to do anything about it.

Crucial Element

Restoring our forests, protecting and reclaiming our topsoil, arresting desert expansion, and protecting the ozone layer will take technological efforts of superhuman dimensions. But all of these efforts will be for naught if the single greatest threat to our planet — the burgeoning population growth — is not arrested. The crucial element in that effort is acceleration of population assistance and voluntary family planning efforts for developing countries.

Congress, which has been the leading player in U.S. international population assistance, needs to restore U.S. leadership in this field. It can do so by setting appropriate funding levels of $500 million per year for the remaining years of this century. The share of the rest of the developed nations would be two billion dollars per year; each of them is already spending more per capita on this issue than the United States is. Foremost in the restoration of U.S. leadership must be the refunding of the United Nations Population Fund (UNFPA), the largest multilateral provider of family planning services. Multilateralism is the way to resolve many of the world's problems. It is now incontrovertible that the multilateral approach has become an indispensable way of running the affairs of the planet.

Demonstrating an unusual fealty to extremists in our society, President Bush vetoed an entire foreign aid appropriations bill because it contained $15 million for the UNFPA for voluntary family planning programs in countries that desperately need even this token assistance and have no one else to turn to. The defunding of UNFPA was an ideological victory handed to a slim but vocal minority in our society which is opposed to medically approved methods (abortion) of family planning. Unable to impose their fanatical anti-family-planning agenda on the American population, this minority group has decided to victimize people who cannot fight back. It looks like an easy win to them, and the fact is that, unless we fight back, hardship and suffering will come to those who rely upon us for help.

Our Very Survival

The very survival of women and children is at stake in this battle. So are the long-term prospects for the ninety nations whose populations can be expected to double in less than thirty years. The short-sighted activities of the present generation are dangerously narrowing the options of our children and grandchildren.

The resources exist to start rebuilding a world that is in ecological and human equilibrium. True equilibrium, as well as true improvement in the quality of all our lives, will happen only when an informed and dedicated population wants it to happen.

How the human species will treat life on earth so as to shape our legacies—good or bad—for all time to come will be settled during most of our lifetimes. The responsibility lies squarely with us. Will future generations praise our foresight or look back in anger and dismay at what we had and lost forever?

10 POPULATION AND THE ENVIRONMENT

POPULATION GROWTH DOES NOT HARM THE ENVIRONMENT

Barry Commoner

Professor Barry Commoner is a prominent biologist and environmentalist and is head of the Center for the Biology of Natural Systems at Queens College in Flushing, New York.

Points to Consider:

1. Why does the author feel that population growth, *per se,* does not harm the environment? Explain.

2. What are economically productive technologies?

3. How can these technologies harm the environment?

4. What does the author propose as a solution? Give an example.

Barry Commoner, "Rapid Population Growth and Environmental Stress", **International Journal of Health Services,** Vol. 21, No. 2, pages 199-227, 1991. © 1991, Baywood Publishing Company, Inc.

Environmental quality. . .is largely governed not by population growth, but by the nature of the technologies of production.

It is useful to begin this article by considering the purpose of analyzing the relation between rapid population growth and environmental quality. One purpose is self-evident: rapid population growth is characteristic of most developing countries and, as a guide to national policy, it is important to determine whether it creates a distinctive impact on the quality of their environment. Another aspect of the issue is more general and the subject of a considerably wider range of discussion. It is concerned with the origin of the environmental crisis: the sharp decline in environmental quality, worldwide, in the last 50 years.

Conventional Wisdom

Some observers have concluded that population growth is the dominant cause of the environmental crisis. The classic statement of this position is Paul Ehrlich's:

"The causal chain of the deterioration [of the environment] is easily followed to its source. Too many cars, too many factories, too much detergent, too much pesticides, multiplying contrails, inadequate sewage treatment plants, too little water, too much carbon dioxide—all can be traced easily to too many people."

If this proposition—that environmental degradation is chiefly a consequence of population growth—were true, the issue under discussion here could be resolved and the operational solution identified: rapid population growth correspondingly intensifies environmental degradation, which must, therefore, be mitigated by reducing the rate of population growth.

Such statements are generally supported by anecdotal data about environmental changes that appear to occur distinctively in countries that have high rates of population growth. Thus, intensive urbanization in Mexico, a country with a 2.6 percent annual rate of population growth in 1980-85, has been accompanied by very high levels of photochemical smog in Mexico City. Similarly, forests have been rapidly destroyed for firewood in countries such as Kenya that have high rates of population growth. However, such anecdotal data are not definitive, for they do not establish a necessary relation between environmental quality and rapid population growth. For example, despite the rapid increase in the population of Mexico City, its photochemical smog level would be much lower if the city had developed an adequate system of electrified mass transit—a well-established technology—as it grew. Similarly, deforestation in Kenya could be greatly diminished if, for example, the rural population, despite the rapid growth, were provided with cooking stoves fired by methane (perhaps produced from sewage or manure) instead of using firewood for that purpose. In both of these cases, the concurrence of rapid population growth and environmental degradation does not necessarily reflect a direct, causal connection between them. Moreover, counter-examples can readily be cited: for example, that Los Angeles or Tokyo, in countries with low rates of population growth, have experienced photochemical smog levels approximating those of Mexico City.

Productive Technologies

Clearly, production technology is a major determinant of economic development. If it also largely determines environmental quality, a crucial question arises: are technologies that are more economically productive always more hazardous to the environment? If so, developing countries must make a cruel choice between environmental quality and economic development. Or, on the contrary, are some production technologies both economically productive and environmentally benign, and therefore a means of solving the environment/development dilemma?

The conventional approach, which is based on the experience of industrialized countries, is that those technologies that are highly productive economically generally have a serious impact on the environment. This leads to the view that developing countries must use such technologies as the means of economic development, and that environmental quality can then be achieved, or at least approached, only by using control devices to minimize their harmful effects. It is this view that has largely governed the introduction of new production technologies in developing countries.

Thus, it can be argued not only that the postwar technologies are faulty environmentally, but that this very failing limits their continued ability to contribute to economic development. It appears, in sum, that the developed nations have been relying on production technologies that are severely limited in their ability to support further economic development because they have harmful effects on the environment.

A Better Approach

It is possible, however, to construct an approach that enhances

73

development without intensifying environmental degradation. The basic precept can be stated quite simply, albeit negatively: developing countries should avoid the production technologies that have characterized the postwar production system in developed countries: centralized power systems, and nuclear power in particular; transportation based on high-compression internal combustion engines; agriculture based on the intensive use of synthetic chemicals; and the petrochemical industry, almost in its entirety (excepting necessary and irreplaceable products such as medicinal drugs). Stated positively, the precept calls for the introduction in developing countries of those new technologies that correct both the environmental and economic defects that have caused so much trouble in the developed countries.

Energy production, which is such a crucial component of economic development, is a useful example of this approach. In those developing countries that have already introduced them, modern energy systems are almost entirely based on the consumption of nonrenewable fuels (chiefly, coal, oil and natural gas); they are also highly centralized, involving, for example, large capital-intensive facilities such as power plants and refineries. These features have generated both environmental and economic difficulties that can be avoided by adopting policies that favor renewable fuels and decentralized systems.

Decentralization

In practice this could be accomplished by a series of linked steps. To begin with, the need for electrical power, at first necessarily based on nonrenewable fuels, could be met by decentralized power plants based on co-generation. Such plants recover both heat and electricity from fuel; they are, therefore, more economical and less polluting than conventional power plants, which waste two-thirds of the fuel's energy in the form of rejected heat. For the sake of efficiency, co-generators must be sized according to the local demand, avoiding the huge investments in a central power plant and its attendant large-scale transmission network. They are therefore decentralized.

Once such a decentralized, energetically and economically efficient energy system is in place, its energy supply can be gradually shifted from nonrenewable to renewable sources. The co-generator's conventional fuel can be replaced by solar fuels: ethanol produced from crops or vegetation, or methane produced from sewage and manure, or from marine algae. Similarly, ethanol and methane can gradually replace nonrenewable motor fuels, and photovoltaic cells can be used to produce electricity, augmented by solar collectors for heat. In each case, these technologies sharply reduce environmental impact, in comparison with the conventional ones. They also cut the cost of energy, and eventually free the economy from the self-destructive effect of the ever-increasing cost of nonrenewable fuels.

The chief conclusion of this analysis of the relation between rapid population growth and environmental quality is that the latter is largely governed not by population growth, but by the nature of the technologies of production. This conclusion links environmental quality directly to the issue that quite properly dominates the concerns of developing countries: economic development. Because of that linkage, these issues are themselves closely related to the problem of population growth.

I refer here to the analysis that offers the best explanation of historic and current population trends: the demographic transition. Briefly stated, this analysis shows that rapid population growth is the natural response to a partial improvement in living standards that reduces the death rate without creating the level of economic security that motivates the next stage of the demographic transition. In this second stage, the birth rate begins to fall, through social effects such as increased education and delayed marriage, and cultural effects such as the influence of reduced infant mortality on fertility. But this has occurred only where standards advance enough to encourage these effects — that is, in developed, industrialized countries. In many developing countries, rapid population growth is largely the unresolved residue of their economic exploitation during the period of colonialism. Deprived of the economic resources needed to raise living standards to levels that allow the second, population-stabilizing phase of the demographic transition, the former colonies suffer through a prolonged period in which their economic development is insufficient to reduce their high rates of population growth. In sum: "Hunger and overpopulation are not ecological manifestations: they are signs of economic and political problems that can be solved humanely, by economic and political means."

Conclusion

Thus, the resolution of the major problems confronted by developing countries—economic development, stabilization of population growth, and environmental quality—all hinge on the proper choice of production technologies. Properly chosen production technologies can improve both economic development and environmental quality. Since by stimulating economic development, such choices will enhance the demographic transition and they will also contribute to the stabilization of the population. This choice is, therefore, a supreme requirement of national policy.

The chemical disaster at Bhopal, India, is only the most dramatic evidence that many of the new industrial technologies are particularly unsuited to developing countries. The trouble arises because modern technological developments are often accepted uncritically as "objectively good", despite the fact that they have been designed with the total well-being of neither industrialized societies nor developing countries in mind. *Appropriate technology* is a concept that ought to be applied everywhere. However, developed countries have a special obligation, for the technological transformation that they must undertake for the sake of environmental quality and long-term economic development is itself well adapted to the needs of developing countries. By initiating this transformation and providing the material resources for poor nations to carry it out, the industrialized countries can properly repay their debt to their former colonies.

RECOGNIZING AUTHOR'S POINT OF VIEW

This activity may be used as an individualized study guide for students in libraries and resource centers or as a discussion catalyst in small group and classroom discussions.

Guidelines

Good readers make clear distinctions between descriptive articles that relate factual information and articles that express a point of view. Articles that express editorial commentary and analysis are featured in this publication. Examine the following statements. Then try to decide if any of these statements take a similar position to any of the authors in Chapter Three. Working as individuals or in small groups, try to match the point of view in each statement below with the most appropriate author in Chapter Three. Mark the appropriate reading number in front of each statement. Mark (O) for any statement that cannot be associated with the point of view of any opinion in Chapter Three.

1. Any discussion of population must include the issue of women's health.

2. Plagues and starvation may be a natural way to limit population.

3. Pollution is a direct result of overpopulation.

4. Governments must allocate resources to curb global population growth.

5. Bad use of modern technology, and not more people, destroys the environment.

6. The less populated industrialized nations use far more than their share of resources.

7. To avoid further environmental damage, we must address social and economic issues of inequality as well as population issues.

8. Local energy production is better for the environment.

9. Overcorwded cities in the next century will mean increased smog, sewage and housing problems.

10. Colonialism is the root cause of today's population problem.

11. Population growth has nothing to do with environmental problems.

12. If we control population growth, we can control environmental destruction.

CHAPTER 4

FEEDING A CROWDED PLANET

MOTHER EARTH CANNOT FEED MORE PEOPLE

Lester R. Brown

Lester R. Brown is president of the Worldwatch Institute and former administrator of the U.S. Department of Agriculture's International Agriculture Development Service.

Points to Consider:

1. What is happening to the world's food supply?

2. How is soil erosion affecting food production?

3. How does population growth affect ozone depletion, global warming and food production?

4. Describe the "social fallout" of rising grain prices.

Lester R. Brown, "Feeding Six Billion", **Worldwatch,** September/October 1989.

Each year, the world's farmers must try to feed 88 million more people with 24 billion fewer tons of topsoil.

Our oldest enemy, hunger, is again at the door. We're exploring the outer reaches of the solar system, reaping the benefits of the computer revolution, and working wonders in medicine, but our ingenuity can't seem to resolve this age-old problem. With more hungry people in the world today than when this decade began, there's little to celebrate on the food front as we enter the nineties.

Between 1986 and 1988, drought-damaged harvests in key producing countries dropped world grain stocks to one of their lowest levels in decades—little more than is necessary to fill the "pipeline" from field to table. As a result, prices increased by nearly half. With higher prices and better weather in 1989, it was widely assumed that production would surge upward and stocks would be rebuilt. But this is not happening.

Rebuilding stocks depends on pushing production above consumption, but this is becoming more difficult. A worldwide scarcity of cropland and irrigation water, combined with a diminishing response to the use of additional chemical fertilizer, is slowing the growth in world food output. Meanwhile, 88 million mouths are added to the world's population each year.

Food scarcity is emerging as the most profound and immediate consequence of global environmental degradation, and it is already affecting the welfare of hundreds of millions of people. The 1988 rise in world grain prices may have been a signal of trouble ahead.

Soil Erosion

Among the environmental trends adversely affecting agriculture, soil erosion tops the list. As the demand for food has risen in recent decades, so have the pressures on the earth's soils. Soil erosion is accelerating as the world's farmers are pressed into plowing highly erodible land, and as traditional rotation systems that maintain soil stability break down.

Some one-third of the world's cropland is losing topsoil at a rate that undermines its future productivity. An estimated 24 billion tons of topsoil washes or blows off the land annually—roughly the amount on Australia's wheatland. Each year, the world's farmers must try to feed 88 million more people with 24 billion fewer tons of topsoil.

This loss is beginning to show up in diminished harvests. Studies undertaken in the U.S. Corn Belt conclude that the loss of one inch of topsoil reduces corn yields from three to six bushels per acre, or an average of six percent. Wheat yields follow a similar pattern.

Soil erosion and cropland loss in Third World nations is intimately linked with another form of environmental degradation: deforestation. As firewood becomes scarce, villagers begin to burn crop residues and animal dung for fuel, depriving the land of organic matter and nutrients. With less organic matter, the soil's ability to absorb and store moisture decreases, making the land more vulnerable to drought. Further, loss of organic matter increases runoff, thus reducing the percolation of rainfall into the subsoil and the recharge of aquifers.

Increased runoff, in turn, leads to flooding. This is now strikingly evident in the Indian subcontinent, where deforestation is destroying tree cover in the Himalayan watersheds. All plants and animals are affected to some degree by the increased exposure to ultraviolet radiation resulting from depletion of the stratospheric ozone layer. This suggests that the worldwide depletion in the ozone layer, roughly three percent over the last two decades, now may be reducing the output of soybeans, the world's leading protein crop.

The effect of hotter summers on world food output can be estimated from the computerized projections of global climate change. As global warming progresses, farm output could be cut sharply in North America and Central Asia, the regions of the earth likely to experience the greatest temperature rise.

The Population Factor

Even while wrestling with the new uncertainties associated with hotter summers, farmers recently learned that they may have to feed more people than they had reckoned. The United Nations Population Fund announced that UN demographers have revised their earlier projections of world population upward, chiefly because of failed family planning efforts. Instead of leveling off at 10 billion, world population will settle at 14 billion. For a world that can't adequately feed 5.2 billion inhabitants today, this comes as sobering news.

In many developing countries, soaring population now has a dual effect on food balance: it increases demand as it degrades the agricultural resource base. For instance, crowded cities and villages create a need for firewood that exceeds the sustainable yield of local forests. Deforestation is the outcome, which in turn increases rainfall runoff and soil erosion. Once started, this vicious cycle is hard to stop. As a result, the agricultural base for hundreds of millions of people is deteriorating on a scale whose consequences are fearful to imagine.

As a result of continuing rapid population growth and slower growth in world grain output, grain production per person has fallen sharply during the late eighties, interrupting the long-term gradual rise since mid-century.

Nowhere to Grow

From the beginning of agriculture until mid-century, growth in the world's cultivated area more or less kept pace with that of population. After that point, the growth in cultivated area slowed to a crawl. After falling in the mid-eighties, it recovered somewhat as the United States returned to production cropland previously idled under farm commodity programs.

Each year, millions of acres of cropland are lost, either because the land is so severely eroded that it is not worth plowing anymore or because of its conversion to non-farm uses, such as construction of new homes, factories and highways. Losses are most pronounced in the densely populated, rapidly industrializing countries of east Asia, including Japan, South Korea, Taiwan and China.

Other densely populated countries that are suffering heavy losses include Egypt, Indonesia, India and Mexico. Both the former Soviet Union and the United States are pulling back from their rapidly eroding land.

Worldwide, the potential for expanding the cultivated area profitably is limited. A few countries, such as Brazil, will be able to add new cropland but, on balance, gains and losses for the nineties will offset each other, as they have during the eighties. Food for the 921 million people to be added during the nineties will have to come from raising land productivity.

The prospect for expanding the irrigated area is only slightly more promising. Several countries, including the United States and China, actually are losing irrigated land as water tables fall and as water is diverted to nonfarm uses. With the net gain in irrigated land estimated at only 59 million acres during the eighties, the supply of irrigation water per person has shrunk by close to eight percent. Although the cropland area per person has been falling steadily for decades, this is the first decade in which both cropland area and irrigation water per person have declined.

The Social Fallout

As grain supplies tighten in more and more countries, world prices will rise. The social effect of rising grain prices is much greater in developing countries than in industrial ones. In the

United States, for example, a $1 loaf of bread contains roughly 5 cents worth of wheat. If the price of wheat were to double, the price of a loaf would increase only to $1.05. However, in developing countries, where wheat is purchased in the market and ground into flour at home, a doubling of retail grain prices translates into a doubling of bread prices. A food-price rise that is merely annoying to the world's affluent can drive consumption below the survival level among the poor.

In Africa, the number of "food insecure" people, defined by the World Bank as those not having enough food for normal health and physical activity, now totals more than 100 million. Some 14.7 million Ethiopians, nearly one-third of the country, are undernourished. Nigeria is close behind, with 13.7 million undernourished people. The Bank summarized the findings of its study by noting that "Africa's food situation is not only serious; it is deteriorating."

An Unpleasant Scenario

The world enters the nineties not only with a low level of grain in reserve, but with little confidence that the "carryover" stocks can be rebuilt quickly. Sketching out the consequences of a poor harvest when stocks are down begins to sound like the social equivalent of science fiction. If the United States were to experience a drought-reduced harvest similar to that of 1988 before stocks are rebuilt, its grain exports would slow to a trickle. By September of that fateful year, the more than 100 countries that import U.S. grain would be competing for meager exportable supplies from Argentina, Australia and France. Fierce competition among importers could double or triple grain prices, driving them far beyond any level previously experienced.

By November, the extent of starvation, food riots and political instability in the Third World would force governments in affluent industrial societies to consider tapping the only remaining food reserve of any size — the 450 million tons of grain fed to livestock. If they decided to restrict livestock feeding and use the grain saved for food relief, governments would have to devise a mechanism for doing so. Would they impose a meat tax to discourage consumption, or would they ration livestock products, much as meat was rationed in many countries during World War II?

Looking at the 90's

Even though projecting food production trends is now a complex undertaking, we do have a model to help us. The recent experience of Japan, where grain yields started rising several decades before those in other countries, offers insight as to how rapidly land productivity might rise for the rest of the world. The world grain yield today, taking into account the wide range of growing conditions, appears to be roughly where Japan's grain yields were in 1970. Since 1970, Japan's rice yield per acre has risen an average of 0.9 percent per year, scarcely half the 1.7 percent annual growth in world population.

The key question for the nineties is whether the world will even be able to match the Japanese. Despite the powerful incentive of domestic price support for their rice pegged at four times the world market, Japanese farmers have run out of agronomic options to achieve major gains in productivity. Farmers in the rest of the world, who are not as skilled, literate or scientifically oriented as are those in Japan, will find it difficult to do better.

If the Japanese agricultural record provides a reasonable sense of what the world can expect during the nineties, and if the world continues with business-as-usual policies in agriculture and family planning, a food emergency within a matter of years may be inevitable. Soaring grain prices and ensuing food riots could both destabilize national governments and threaten the integrity of the international monetary system.

Barring any dramatic technological breakthroughs on the food front, the gap between population growth and food production will widen. Avoiding a life-threatening food situation during the nineties may depend on quickly slowing world population growth to bring it in line with food output. The only reasonable goal will be to try to cut it in half by the end of the century, essentially doing what Japan did in the fifties and what China did in the seventies.

The time may have come for world leaders to issue a call to action. It may now be appropriate for the United Nations secretary general, the president of the World Bank, and national political leaders to urge couples everywhere to stop at two surviving children. Difficult and harsh though this may seem, bringing population and food into balance by lowering birthrates is surely preferable to doing so inadvertently by allowing death rates to rise.

12 FEEDING A CROWDED PLANET

MOTHER EARTH CAN FEED BILLIONS MORE

Dennis T. Avery

Dennis Avery is a fellow of the Hudson Institute in Indianapolis and principal author of the Institute's 1991 book, Global Food Progress 1991.

Points to Consider:

1. How can the world feed another four billion people?

2. What has happened to per-capita food supplies since 1960?

3. Describe how the environmental threat is exaggerated.

4. How is fear used by population-control advocates?

The globe could feed another two billion people right now. . . .We could feed four billion more people if the Third World fully adopted the latest high-yield farm technologies.

As the United Nations General Assembly opened in December 1991, the U.S. Congress dared President Bush to veto renewed funding for the U.N.'s Family Planning Agency. Senator Brock Adams (D., Wash.) spoke for the Senate majority when he said, "We simply cannot continue to have more and more people and fewer and fewer resources and not expect the famines, the hunger and starvation."

Plenty of Food

There's just one problem with the senator's rationale: the world isn't running out of food or farming resources. The globe could feed another two billion people right now mainly on the good land diverted from crops by government policies in the U.S. and Argentina.

We could feed four billion more people if the Third World fully adopted the latest high-yield farm technologies—including hybrid rice, high-protein corn and acid-tolerant seed varieties for a billion acres of currently barren acid soil savannahs.

Public TV's "Race to Save the Planet" series says flatly that world food production is falling behind population growth. This isn't so. Per-capita food supplies in the Third World have increased 25 percent above subsistence since 1960—during the peak of the current population growth surge. The U.S. Agency for International Development's newly completed demographic survey shows Third World birth rates slowing more rapidly than anyone had predicted. And Third World food production continues to rise twice as fast as its population.

Congressmen make headlines with overseas trips to "fight hunger". But to find famine today, they have to go to an African country experiencing both drought and war. The threat of severe hunger, which once faced perhaps a half of the world's population on a frequent basis, now threatens perhaps three percent to five percent in most years. And even Africa is now getting high-yielding crop varieties and farming systems, after a late start in farm research.

The Natural Resources Defense Council says that we need a "chemical free" agriculture to protect wildlife. But without science-based agriculture we'd already have plowed under

another 10 million square miles of wildlife habitat for food. Instead, because we have raised yields on existing cropland — with better seeds, irrigation, fertilizer and pest control — we're feeding twice as many people on the same farm land we used in 1960.

Today's crop pesticides pose little danger to humans or wildlife. Their residues are less toxic than mustard or pickles. DDT is long gone; the new compounds use a few ounces per acre instead of pounds, degrade in hours or days, and target narrowly on insects and weeds. Fertilizer is no threat to anything when used moderately to replace nutrients taken up by crops.

New Technologies

Lester Brown, editor of *Worldwatch* magazine, says the big food gains are an "illusion of progress" produced by destroying topsoil and mining groundwater. But he doesn't tell us about the new conservation technologies:

- "Conservation tillage" systems halve soil-erosion rates on hundreds of millions of acres in North America and

Western Europe.

- In West Africa, a new system called "alley cropping" eliminates much of the need for slash-and-burn farming.
- In the Amazon rain forest, a legume called *kudzu* can cut the environmental impact of slash-and burn farming 90 percent.
- Farmers waste a third of the world's water with flood irrigation. New sprinkler, drip and trailing-tube irrigation systems could double water-use efficiency. In fact, the world's worst soil erosion problems are in the regions trying to feed more people with traditional agriculture.

Some agriculturists warn that existing farm technologies have been "used up". But other researchers are just beginning to harness the awesome power of genetic engineering:

- Engineering more growth hormone in a hog's system can give us pork with one-third less fat, produced with one-fourth less feed grain. In effect, the growth hormone will manufacture 30 million to 40 million tons of feed corn a year from laboratory bacteria.
- Cloning and tissue culture have produced a revolution in tree breeding, typically raising yields fourfold. Thus the forest products we need can be produced on less acreage.

The reality of the world's food and environmental gains are confirmed by all the major published data series, including the UN's Food and Agriculture Organization, and the U.S. Department of Agriculture. Every reputable study of the world's "carrying capacity" has concluded that the world can feed its expected population growth.

The job won't be easy: it will take continuing, and broadening, investments in agricultural research and infrastructure. Even more important will be good economic policies in Third World countries. But the evidence argues convincingly that the job can be done.

Where are the headlines trumpeting this good news? Where are the interviews with enthusiastic international scientists? Where are the features about Tanzania doubling its grain production? Instead, we get sermons on the need for organic farming—which is not yet a success. The zealots pushing wilderness and zero population growth have been far too willing to indict farm science as irrelevant and/or dangerous. They're trying to back us into an intellectual corner from which economic stagnation and population suppression will seem the only escape.

At the same time, the decline of public confidence in the "establishment" has left agricultural science with precious few defenders. After all, most of the new food-production wonders were developed by big corporations, labs and governments.

Farmers won't make the defense. They like new technology, but only if it adds to their profits. They dislike new technology if it permits farmers in other countries to produce more — and that is happening as farm technology spreads overseas.

The science establishment has certainly made no efforts to shoot down the fear-mongers. Some researchers actually welcome the phony famine predictions on the theory that famine fears would generate more research funds. Instead, the famine activists have shifted public funding away from real agricultural research toward organic farming and population management.

Fear Campaigns

The public, no longer willing to believe the Agriculture Department, the Food and Drug Administration or the local university's entomology department, is now at the mercy of a gleeful troupe of media performers. These activists are capitalizing on memberships, newsletters, donations, books and public-policy campaigns.

Food is usually part of the fear campaigns, because food is so basic to our lives. So far, scientists have played into the fear-monger's hands. Good scientists disapprove of headline-hunting and never develop the skill. Ironically, famine-mongering and environmental activism may now lead to more hunger and more environmental losses. If the claims of poisoned wildlife and lost genetic diversity convince the general public that farm science is bad, we could lose the momentum of our agricultural research. That would mean slower progress against hunger, and slower world economic growth. It would also threaten the environment and wildlife far more drastically than pesticides.

The world's farm resource demands are rising even more rapidly than the famine-mongers have warned us. In the 1990s, population growth will raise world food demand about 18 percent. But income-driven diet improvements will raise the demands on world agricultural resources an additional 20 to 30 percent. Total farm resource demand could increase 30 to 50 percent, just in the 1990s.

Without still more gains in farm productivity, that rising demand will translate directly into environmental stress. Third World people are still driven by a fierce desire to live and eat better. If that means using fragile semi-arid farm land more intensely, so be it.

The environmental struggle won't be won or lost in Boston or Iowa. It will be won or lost in the densely populated countries of Asia. Since a better diet is the first goal of people gaining affluence, a continuing flow of agricultural technology is now especially critical to environmental sustainability. But if we continue to be misled on hunger, we may not have solutions to offer.

13   FEEDING A CROWDED PLANET

BIOTECHNOLOGY WILL PRODUCE MORE FOOD

Luther Val Giddings

Luther Val Giddings, PhD., was a Biotechnology Consultant for the Agriculture and Rural Development branch of the World Bank when he wrote this article.

Points to Consider:

1. How many people could theoretically be fed by advances in biotechnology?

2. What is RFLP mapping? How will it increase food production?

3. What are the environmental advantages of biotechnology?

4. How can biotechnology help control population growth?

Excerpted from testimony by Luther Val Giddings before the U.S. House Committee on Science, Space and Technology, February 23, 1989.

The productivity increases that will be possible in the next decade or two could feed a world population of 10 billion. . .it is theoretically possible.

There is no question that the techniques of modern biotechnology will lead to increases in food production. These are most likely to come through the use of newly improved strains of existing crops, or increased use of previously under-utilized crops, though biotechnology will also make some contributions in terms of more intensive farming methods and techniques. No reasonable person familiar with biotechnology or agriculture doubts that there is enormous potential here.

Food Productivity Increases

Many discussions of the degree to which the new biotechnologies could contribute to productivity increases fail to take proper note of the enormous gains in agricultural productivity over the past 40 years. Since 1950, world agricultural output has increased at a compound annual rate of 2.43 percent.

Future increases in food production will come both in animal husbandry and in the raising of crops. These increases will be based on increases in absolute rates of production as well as improvements in production efficiency. The techniques of modern biotechnology will contribute directly and indirectly, but at the same time advances will come also through incremental improvements in production methods from more traditional or classical approaches, as they have at a regular rate since the end of World War II.

One of the elegant new ways in which progress will be made is illustrated by the work of Roger Beachy and his colleagues at Washington University in St. Louis. In the course of studying viral diseases of plants, they have produced a technique called engineered viral cross-protection. Through a mechanism not yet well understood, this inhibits the development of disease symptoms in the plant when it is subsequently infected with a virus that would normally weaken or kill the plant, causing large losses in yield. As annual losses of food crops to such viral diseases can approach 50 percent in some tropical countries, the potential for improving productivity is apparent.

An even more powerful source of productivity increases can be found in a technique that is called RFLP mapping. This procedure enables biologists to identify genetic markers

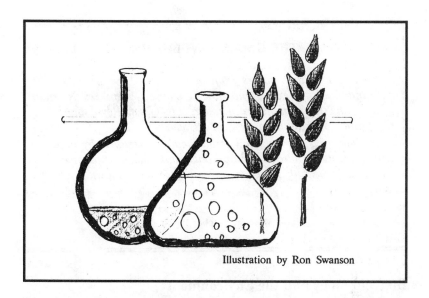

Illustration by Ron Swanson

distributed randomly throughout an organism's genetic material.

It means that scientists can now combine the powerful tools of modern genetic engineering with sophisticated computer analyses. For example, scientists have identified six genes that have a major impact on flavor in tomatoes. They have used this information to produce a new variety of tomato with enhanced flavor that should be available to growers for the coming season. Similar progress has been achieved with respect to genes controlling water metabolism (which will have an impact on both drought resistance and suitability for canning) and insect resistance.

All this has been accomplished simply by monitoring and selecting the results of test crosses with these new information technologies. No genetic engineering of the tomato plant, *per se,* was involved. Similar work is being pursued with corn, cabbage, onion, sugarbeets, roses, azaleas, alfalfa, and other plants. Such work is not yet far advanced with any agricultural animal, however, although the potential for advances is similar.

The beauty of this technology is that it is a straightforward matter to apply it to almost any plant or animal that can be bred in captivity. Once the genetic markers are identified, they can be used as tools to monitor and manipulate selective breeding programs to take full advantage of the existing pools of genetic variation in agricultural species.

Bread for billions comes from the multiplied yields of farmers in China, India, Mexico, and other countries where Dr. Norman Borlaug, the Iowa plant breeder, and the Green Revolution have transformed agriculture in the past 30 years.

Borlaug says Africa's soil fertility can be restored by applying such nutrients as nitrogen, phosphorus, and potash. It takes money and skill, but South Africa and Zimbabwe have shown it can be done.

Richard Critchfield, **World Monitor,** October 1990

Biotechnology and the Environment

While factors other than population growth affect the environment, population growth compounds these effects. The prospect that advances in biotechnology might break, or at least attenuate the cycle of positive feedback between the problems of population growth and environmental degradation has not been thoroughly explored to date. There are several promising indications, however. Contributions might come in at least two general areas: production of plants (both food crops and trees) better able to resist drought, saline, or other environmental stresses such as extremes of temperature or poor soil quality; and the replacement of existing agriculture practices with developments or refinements that are more environmentally benign. An example of the latter might be found if the generation of crops resistant to environmentally acceptable herbicides leads to retiring from use those herbicides that are more persistent or toxic.

Biotechnology could be something of a two-edged sword here, however: not all that is possible with biotechnology will be environmentally benign. In fact, negative environmental consequences could well result from poorly thought-out applications of the new technologies, although it is not reasonable to view these as intrinsic to use of the technologies *per se.* Forage grasses capable of flourishing in poor tropical soils, for example, would enable more tropical rain forest to be converted to cattle pastures with slightly less destructive results than at present. But the last thing we need are any further stimuli for cattle farming in the tropics, as cattle are among the least efficient converters of plant biomass to animal protein, independent of the irreparable harm being done to tropical rain forests.

Human Fertility

One area in which valuable contributions from biotechnology might be anticipated is in the management of human fertility. There is an urgent need for appropriate contraceptive technologies, particularly ones that could be coupled with advances in child care in developing countries that would help break the link between fertility and immediate economic advantage. This is an area that has been disproportionately underfunded in industrial countries, especially in the past eight years, as U.S. policy in this area has been co-opted by individuals holding a narrow, sectarian point of view that neither represents American public opinion at large nor reflects a rational assessment of global realities.

14 FEEDING A CROWDED PLANET

BIOTECHNOLOGY IS NO MIRACLE CURE

John E. Young and Lester R. Brown

Lester R. Brown is president of Worldwatch Institute. This reading by Brown and Worldwatch staff member John Young was taken from a chapter on world food production in the Worldwatch Institute's publication entitled State of the World — 1990.

Points to Consider:

1. Why is biotechnology difficult to apply to crop production?

2. How is money a limit to biotechnology?

3. Why is traditional farming better in the Third World?

4. What other limits are there to biotechnology?

Lester R. Brown and John E. Young, **State of the World—1990**, W. W. Norton and Company, 1990.

Plants—the ultimate source of all food—have been far less responsive to biotechnological manipulation.

Grandiose claims about biotechnology and food production have been common since the first successful attempts at genetic engineering in the early seventies. As recently as 1984, one writer predicted that "in five to 10 years, Saudi Arabia may look like the wheat fields of Kansas." The unfortunate reality in 1989—when Kansas lost over a third of its wheat crop to drought—was that the wheat fields of Kansas came to resemble the still-fallow Saudi Arabian desert. Biotechnology has proven more difficult to apply to agriculture than its champions expected.

Agricultural Limits

It is difficult to overstate the revolutionary nature of the biological discoveries of the last two decades. The assortment of techniques referred to as biotechnology is opening new frontiers in areas from manufacturing to health care to pollution cleanup.

Genetic engineering—the direct transfer of genes, which encode all life process, from one organism to another—is the best-known and most fundamental of the new biological techniques.

Animal biotechnology has moved forward quickly because much more is known about the basic cell processes of animals than of plants, and because human health products are usually tested first in animals. Although the social impacts, safety, and long-term performance of some of the new animal biotechnologies are quite controversial, they are advancing rapidly, with some already commercialized.

But plants—the ultimate source of all food—have been far less responsive to biotechnological manipulation. From the outset, it was molecular biologists and other scientists unfamiliar with agriculture and plant breeding who were most bullish on crop biotechnology. Most agricultural scientists have rightly remained skeptical.

Dr. Norman Borlaug, the plant breeder whose high-yielding wheats won him a Nobel Prize, recently pointed out that "the most productive applications of biotechnology and molecular genetics, in the near term, appear to be in medicine, animal sciences, and microbiology. . . .It will likely take considerably longer to develop biotechnological research techniques that will dramatically improve the production of our major crop species."

Cereals—like all grasses—have been particularly resistant to genetic manipulation: they are not compatible with the bacterium most commonly used to introduce foreign genes into plant cells, and they are difficult to regenerate from altered cells.

Furthermore, once genes are transferred, conventional breeding techniques must still be used to evaluate the altered plants and make them suitable for distribution to farmers or for further breeding. The entire process—from gene transfer to dissemination of a new variety—can take as long as conventional breeding (typically five-15 years). The new biotechnologies will allow scientists to specify the genetic structure of plants with increasing precision, but they will complement—not replace—plant breeding.

A Matter of Money

But it takes money to move genes. Economics and national and international policies will determine whether biotechnology can achieve its technical potential to provide more food for a hungry world.

Most of the money now going into biotechnology research

comes not from public or philanthropic organizations but from multinational corporations. In the United States, industry spent an estimated $300 million on agricultural biotechnology research in 1987. The U.S. Department of Agriculture spent $85 million on such work in the same year.

U.S. biotechnology companies are fond of describing miracle crops that will feed hungry millions, and often use the promise of such immense benefits to attract investors and justify minimal regulation. But the application of biotechnology in the rich nations may not yield the rather prosaic miracles needed by small farmers in developing countries. Corporations will use biotechnology to develop crops and agricultural products they expect to be profitable and, if possible, which they can patent. Much of their effort, for example, is now focused on fruits and vegetables and on expensive flavoring and sweetener crops.

Several of the larger agrichemical firms see the most potential profit in selling farmers integrated packages of seeds, fertilizer, and pesticides. In conjunction with subsidiary or affiliated seed companies, they are combining research on chemicals and plants, developing crop varieties that will be compatible with their own products. Although pest and disease resistance are commonly touted as major goals in corporate crop development programs, resistance to herbicides—which will in fact increase the use of these chemicals—is receiving R&D priority.

Third World Limits

Chemical herbicides substitute for tillage (plowing), the traditional method of controlling weeds; they increase crop yields only if previous weed control methods were inadequate. No-till farming—which means fewer tractor trips through a farmer's field—can substantially reduce fuel use and soil erosion, but its reliance on herbicides poses greater risk of contaminated groundwater and adverse effects on wildlife. Some herbicides are toxic or carcinogenic, and questions remain about the safety of even the "new-generation" herbicides.

Moreover, herbicides offer little to farmers in developing countries, where most of the world's hungry people live. Hand weeding is cheaper, because labor is both abundant and inexpensive, and it is safer than using chemicals. Herbicides make economic sense in high-capital agriculture and when labor costs are high; in most poor country farming areas, the opposite situation exists.

Similarly, bovine growth hormone (BGH)—one of the first animal biotechnology products to be commercialized, and one that can increase cows' milk production by as much as 10-25 percent—is not a practical technology for most livestock owners in the Third World. At roughly $100 per cow, BGH will cost as much per year as many people in developing countries spend on food.

Doubts

Controversy over genetic resources and their control could impede the development of biotechnology for developing countries. Realizing that the genes from native plants may be used to develop substitutes for their exports or be sold back to them in new products at high prices, developing countries have become understandably reluctant to allow unrestricted access to their genetic heritage. Though direct compensation schemes may be impractical, it is only just that industrial nations support development of biotechnology to feed the Third World—in full partnership with those countries.

Furthermore, all private and public efforts in biotechnology will be undermined if the current wave of plant and animal extinctions goes unchecked. If the diversity of both crop and noncrop species is not safeguarded, much of the raw material now available for genetic manipulation will be lost. Biotechnology can move genes, but its ability to create them is virtually nonexistent.

WHAT IS EDITORIAL BIAS?

This activity may be used as an individualized study guide for students in libraries and resource centers or as a discussion catalyst in small group and classroom discussions.

The capacity to recognize an author's point of view is an essential reading skill. The skill to read with insight and understanding involves the ability to detect different kinds of opinions or bias. **Sex bias, race bias, ethnocentric bias, political bias and religious bias** *are five basic kinds of opinions expressed in editorials and all literature that attempts to persuade. They are briefly defined in the glossary below.*

GLOSSARY OF TERMS FOR READING SKILLS

Sex Bias—the expression of dislike for and/or feeling of superiority over the opposite sex or a particular sexual minority

Race Bias—The expression of dislike for and/or feeling of superiority over a racial group

Ethnocentric Bias—the expression of a belief that one's own group, race, religion, culture or nation is superior. Ethnocentric persons judge others by their own standards and values.

Political Bias—the expression of political opinions and attitudes about domestic or foreign affairs

Religious Bias—the expression of a religious belief or attitude

---

Guidelines

1. From the readings in Chapter Four, locate five sentences that provide examples of *editorial opinion* or *bias.*

2. Write down each of the above sentences and determine what kind of bias each sentence represents. Is it *sex bias, race bias, ethnocentric bias, political bias* or *religious bias*?

3. Make up-one sentence statements that would be an example of each of the five types of editorial bias listed above.

4. See if you can locate one factual statement from each reading in Chapter Four.

CHAPTER 5

POPULATION CONTROL AND SOCIAL JUSTICE

15 POPULATION CONTROL AND SOCIAL JUSTICE

ABORTION MUST BE A PART OF POPULATION CONTROL POLICY

Chet Atkins

Chet Atkins is a U.S. Congressman from the State of Massachusetts.

Points to Consider:

1. How is family planning linked to survival of the planet?

2. How does the "Mexico City" policy make "war" on women?

3. Why is abortion a way of life for some women in poor nations?

4. Why should the "Mexico City" policy be reversed?

Excerpted from the testimony of Chet Atkins before the House Subcommittee on International Operations of the Committee on Foreign Affairs, June 4, 1991.

This policy has completely failed to accomplish anything other than confuse and frustrate global family planning efforts.

In 1984, America's historic role as a leading world voice on family planning issues became a whisper. At the world conference on population in Mexico City that year, the United States introduced a new policy that is now known as the "Mexico City Policy". In its "white paper" describing this policy, the Reagan administration took flight from reality when it said, I quote: "Population growth is, of itself, a neutral phenomenon. The relationship between population growth and economic development is not a negative one." The Mexico City policy prohibits the United States from funding organizations that choose to counsel women about abortion as part of their range of family planning services, and organizations that perform abortion services using non-U.S. funds.

Ignoring Growth

Sadly, the Mexico City policy is not without successes. The United States has succeeded in completely ignoring rapid world population growth and the devastating effect that it is having on our environment, we have succeeded in defunding the most respected and effective international family planning organizations in the world, and we have succeeded in miring the international family planning community in a sea of bureaucratic entanglement. This is hardly a record of which we should be proud.

To say that the global community as a whole has not made progress in slowing population growth and increasing contraceptive use rates would be inaccurate. However, these strides have been made in spite of U.S. policy, not because of it. In 1989, this subcommittee held a hearing to determine the precise effects of the Mexico City policy on international family planning. We discovered that many of the organizations that were taking U.S. funds were over-complying with the Mexico City policy for fear of losing U.S. dollars. Many organizations stopped collecting data on abortion, and other organizations stopped biomedical research on contraceptives. While it is easy to say on paper that "promotion" of abortion is prohibited, it is virtually impossible to determine the scope of this prohibition in the real world.

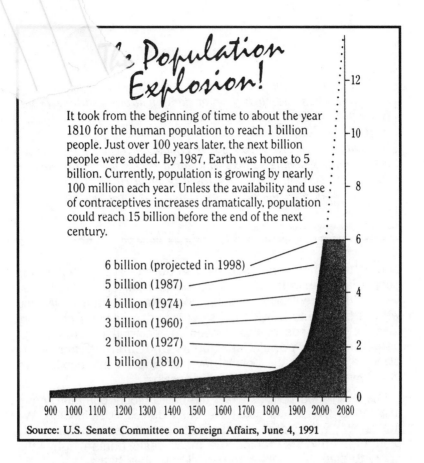

Population Explosion!

It took from the beginning of time to about the year 1810 for the human population to reach 1 billion people. Just over 100 years later, the next billion people were added. By 1987, Earth was home to 5 billion. Currently, population is growing by nearly 100 million each year. Unless the availability and use of contraceptives increases dramatically, population could reach 15 billion before the end of the next century.

6 billion (projected in 1998)
5 billion (1987)
4 billion (1974)
3 billion (1960)
2 billion (1927)
1 billion (1810)

900 1000 1100 1200 1300 1400 1500 1600 1700 1800 1900 2000 2080

Source: U.S. Senate Committee on Foreign Affairs, June 4, 1991

The Larger Scope

This hearing also provided revealing information about the larger scope of global family planning. Now more than ever it is critical that we recognize the link between family planning and the sustenance of life on this planet. Since the 1989 hearing on the Mexico City policy, the population of the earth has increased by 200 million people. Also within this time frame, we have destroyed almost 50 million acres of tropical rain forests, and we have lost almost 30 million acres of land to desertification. According to the World Health Organization, one woman dies each minute of each day as the result of pregnancies that their bodies were either too weak, malnourished, diseased, or simply too young to handle. Explain to these women that population growth is a neutral phenomenon.

Within the next generation, three billion young people will enter their reproductive years. This represents the largest "baby boom" that the planet has ever endured—a full 700 million people larger than the last generation to enter their reproductive years. The current level of global commitment to family planning will not be able to provide the resources and services necessary to meet the needs of this generation. Without a restored U.S. commitment to population studies and international family planning, reaching the optimal level of global contraceptive use in the twenty-first century will be impossible.

Our misguided policies affect the entire global community, not just the organizations that have been denied U.S. funding. We are at war with women in developing nations. Without family planning, they are denied the most basic human right—the ability to plan the number and spacing of their births.

A Fact of Life

At the 1989 hearing, we heard the story of a pregnant woman in Turkey who could not understand our moral dilemma about abortion; to her it was a fact of life. Without access to family planning she became pregnant. She could not bear to watch another one of her children starve, so she dealt with the problem in the only way she knew how—using a chicken feather to self-induce an abortion.

There was also the woman in Bangladesh who worked at a U.S. funded family planning clinic. She stated that if a woman, bleeding and doubled over in pain resulting from a botched abortion, entered her clinic, she would have to turn her away. "We can't touch abortion; we can't tell her anything. She just has to go away."

Most women in the developing world are denied the ability to control the number and spacing of their births. Through the Mexico City policy, we support this unconscionable burden on women. This policy forces us to deny funding to the very organizations that can give women the ability to plan their births.

Finally, through our ambivalence toward international family planning, we promote environmental degradation. The Earth is hard pressed to cope with growing population pressures. On a daily basis we are confronted with new horror stories about global warming, coastal overfishing, and water depletion, to name a few. And, on a daily basis, we remain blissfully ignorant of the root cause of most environmental degradation — global overpopulation.

Reversing Our Policy

In 1989, the United Nations held an international forum on population in Amsterdam. At this forum, 79 nations came together to formulate a global population agenda. The United States sent a delegation to this forum, but they stood in the shadows of the forum. We were shackled by the Mexico City policy, unable to make any meaningful commitments to the other nations in attendance.

In 1994, the United Nations will hold another international forum on population; whether the United States will be a leader or a disinterested observer at this forum will depend on whether we are willing to reverse the Mexico City policy. This policy has completely failed to accomplish anything other than confuse and frustrate global family planning efforts. We have forced clinics to comply with regulations stricter than the laws of their nation in order to receive U.S. funding, and we have refused to fund competent, respected organizations, simply because they choose to answer women's questions about abortion in countries where abortion is a legal option.

16 POPULATION CONTROL AND SOCIAL JUSTICE

ABORTION MUST NOT BE A PART OF POPULATION CONTROL POLICY

Richard Doerflinger

Richard Doerflinger is Associate Director for Policy Development of the National Conference of Catholic Bishops.

Points to Consider:

1. How does the author feel that abortion actually undermines family planning programs?

2. Why is Pathfinders clinic in West Java so deplorable?

3. Why must abortion and family planning be separated?

4. What provision of the "Mexico City" policy is now under attack? Why?

Excerpted from the testimony of Richard Doerflinger before the House Subcommittee on International Operations of the Committee on Foreign Affairs, June 4, 1991.

The inclusion of abortion in any family planning program undermines the program's goal of preventing unintended pregnancies.

The question raised by the Mexico City policy is essentially the same as the question raised by the domestic Title X regulations recently upheld by the U.S. Supreme Court: should the United States insist that non-governmental organizations receiving U.S. government funds refrain from performing and promoting abortion as a family planning method? We believe the answer to this question is yes, for several reasons.

The Abortion Question

First, a pragmatic reason: there is ample evidence that the inclusion of abortion in any family planning program undermines the program's goal of preventing unintended pregnancies. Or conversely, restricting access to abortion decreases unintended pregnancies. This has long been known, and was one of Congress's stated reasons for denying funding to abortion-related programs in the Title X statute of 1970.

In short, if you want to reduce unintended pregnancies, the last thing you want to do — or rather, the one thing you never want to do — is subsidize groups that provide or promote abortion in their family planning programs.

Second, the policy is needed precisely because so many non-governmental organizations, when left to their own devices, simply ignore their own research findings and refuse to recognize any difference at all between family planning and abortion. Planned Parenthood's declarations that abortion is simply a "back-up" method of birth control are well known. Another example can be found in the August 1990 newsletter of the Pathfinder Fund. Pathfinder has announced that it is using a new grant from the Brush Foundation to "collaborate with Indonesian Planned Parenthood Association (IPPA) to help them establish a comprehensive family planning clinic in Bandung, West Java. This new clinic will provide a full range of contraceptive services, including male and female sterilization and early abortion services. The clinic hopes to "provide early abortion services to 515 women" in its first year of operation.

Not mentioned by Pathfinder, but easily learned by perusing the Alan Guttmacher Institute's most recent overview of national abortion policies, is the fact that Indonesian law bans abortion except to save the mother's life. Pathfinder will be using its grant

113

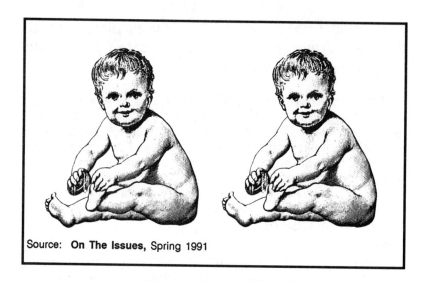

Source: **On The Issues,** Spring 1991

not only to undermine the purported goal of its own family planning program, but also to evade the laws of the sovereign nation in which it is a guest. If not for the Mexico City policy, Pathfinder could be using not only private foundation money, but U.S. government funds to establish such deplorable programs.

Lack of Support

This brings me to a third reason: use of abortion as a method of birth control does not have wide public support either in the United States or abroad. In the U.S., opinion polls show close to 90 percent opposition to the use of abortion for this purpose. A recent Wirthlin poll shows most Americans favoring a legal ban on abortion except to save the mother's life or in cases of rape or incest—and these are the cases in which abortions are allowed under the Mexico City policy itself. If anything, opposition to abortion in developing nations is even stronger; almost all these nations legally prohibit the use of abortion as a mere back-up to contraceptive failure.

Increasingly, this is becoming true in Europe as well. Most of the new democracies breaking away from the Soviet orbit have begun to move away from the old Stalinist policy that treated abortion as a method of birth control. Czechoslovakia, Hungary, Poland and Yugoslavia have all taken steps toward more respectful treatment of the unborn.

RESPECT FOR LIFE

In a modern society scarred by "violence, abortion, euthanasia, the marginalization of the disabled and the poor," the Pope said, "it is the woman who is called to keep alive the spark of life, the respect for the mystery of all new life."

"Society is more sensitive every day to the rights of the child," the Pope said. But he warned that any child is nevertheless still a potential victim of a long list of ills, including "the evil of a part of society that makes attempts on his life even before birth through the practice of abortion."

Excerpted from a speech by Pope John Paul II in Mexico City, **Los Angeles Times,** May 11, 1990

A Simple Distinction

Last, but certainly not least, is the fact that the separation between abortion and family planning is good common sense and good morality. Numerous international declarations on human rights and on medical ethics underscore this simple distinction, by recognizing the already conceived child in the womb as a member of the human family deserving care and protection.

Even Planned Parenthood once recognized this distinction, stating in its 1963 educational brochures that birth control "merely postpones the beginning of life" while "abortion kills the life of a baby after it has begun." As recently as February 1989, Planned Parenthood materials on the Title X family planning program recognized and accepted the program's disparate treatment of contraception and abortion:

"The purpose of Title X is simple: the provision of contraceptive services and information in order to help lower the incidence of unintended pregnancy, to improve maternal health by doing so, and to prevent recourse to abortion. That was its original purpose, and that is still its purpose today."

Obviously, a program whose purpose is to prevent recourse to abortion cannot also have the purpose of facilitating and promoting recourse to abortion. Those who would deny this simple fact are straining logic and common sense.

Is rapid population growth a potentially serious world

problem? If so, do programs of family planning offer the best way to address this problem? Must the United States and other nations act more aggressively to protect our fragile environment so as to avert an ecological disaster? These are all enormously complex questions, worthy of long study and debate, and many thoughtful people find them more difficult to answer with a simple "yes" or "no" the more they know about these subjects. But all these questions share one thing in common: none of them is the question posed by the Mexico City policy or the effort to rescind it.

In fact, individuals and organizations defending the Mexico City policy hold a wide array of opinions on these other issues. The National Right to Life Committee, for example, raised no objection last year to the $60 million boost given to population assistance—so long as the funds would be used by family planning organizations rather than by organizations promoting abortion.

Family Disruption

Independently of the United States, the delegation from the Holy See (the Vatican) proposed a resolution stating that abortion should not be treated as a method of family planning; the U.S. delegation supported this resolution, as did Norway, France, Italy, West Germany, and the great majority of developing nations. The Conference's final consensus statement urged governments to "take appropriate steps to help women avoid abortion, which in no case should be promoted as a method of family planning." At the U.S. delegation's suggestion, the statement added that governments should, "wherever possible, provide for the humane treatment and counseling of women who have had recourse to abortion."

The United States acted in harmony with this statement of the assembled member nations of the UN by announcing that non-governmental organizations receiving U.S. funds would have to abide by the UN policy. This practice of excluding abortion from family planning while improving care and treatment for women who have had abortions is the "Mexico City" policy now under attack in Congress.

No bill designed to reverse the Mexico City policy can by any stretch of the imagination be called a "Family Planning Protection Act". Since inclusion of abortion in a family planning program only undermines the purpose, integrity and basic logic of the program, such a bill should be called either the "Abortion Promotion Act" or the "Family Planning Disruption Act".

17 POPULATION CONTROL AND SOCIAL JUSTICE

CHINA'S "ONE-CHILD" PROGRAM: AN OVERVIEW

Jodi L. Jacobson

Jodi L. Jacobson, a senior researcher at the Worldwatch Institute, *is working on population and development issues.*

Points to Consider:

1. How does China promote population control?

2. Has the program worked?

3. Why are boys considered "big happiness"?

4. What are the four modernizations, and how do they relate to China's one-child policy?

Jodi L. Jacobson, "Baby Budget", **Worldwatch**, September/October 1989.

Where women are caught between the demands of the state to limit fertility and the demands of the husband's family to bear a son, violence against both mothers and first-born daughters has increased.

China's most recent experiment in social engineering—reducing population growth by promoting one-child families—is nothing less than an unprecedented attempt to change the reproductive behavior of an entire nation. Taking to population planning with characteristic zeal, the revolutionary government has, for the past decade, strongly encouraged couples to limit themselves to one child. However, achieving the goal of zero population growth by early in the next century is proving to be a Herculean task, even for the Chinese.

In strictly demographic terms, China already is a family-planning success story. Sharp reductions in fertility since the sixties have put the country farther down the road toward a stable population size than most other Third World nations. Today, however, due to the legacy of past growth, the share of people of reproductive age in China is large and growing, indicating that the population will continue to expand for at least three decades. Even at its current low level of fertility, China's population will exceed 1.5 billion by 2020.

Hot Debate

The one-child policy, without a doubt the most hotly debated family planning strategy in the world, has been criticized on a number of grounds. First, it is (at least on some levels) a compulsory program in a world where even voluntary family planning remains controversial. Second, with one-child families, the next generation of elderly will have far fewer laborers to support it, raising questions about how China will provide old-age security. Third, the policy's immediate economic benefits to the largely rural populace remain unclear.

Although alternatives to the one-child program that might meet China's population goals and lessen the growing opposition to current policy have not been universally adopted, there is some evidence that new, more lenient approaches to population planning are being tried in a majority of provinces. Nevertheless, over the next several years, China will face a choice between allowing a slightly higher rate of population growth (and, perhaps, the addition of another 100 million to its population) or resorting to more stringent and compulsory measures to restrain

Chinese Government poster encouraging the one-child family. Sketch by Ron Swanson

fertility.

Today, China's leaders follow the population's upward climb with the nervous air of an expectant father. Their apprehensions are justifiable. With 1.1 billion people and counting, China may already have reached its environmental limits.

The threat that population growth will unravel past gains and halt further development understandably preoccupies the Chinese. Life for the average Chinese person has improved markedly since the birth of the People's Republic in 1949, at least in terms of health, nutrition and life expectancy. As in most developing nations, though, population pressures in China threaten to undermine hard-won advances in meeting social needs. And resources—forests, land and water—are already stretched thin.

One Is Best

Prior to 1970, official support for family planning was sporadic at best. In the early seventies, with the Chinese population well on its way to one billion, the government recognized the need to reduce fertility and slow growth to reduce pressure on natural resources. The state family planning agency began to promote a policy known as *wan-xi-shao*, literally "later-longer-fewer". The policy encouraged Chinese couples to marry later than the average age of 20, to lengthen the amount of time between first and subsequent births, and to have fewer children overall.

In 1979, a new slogan, "one is best, at most two, never a third," subtly reflected yet another change in the country's demographic goals—the shift to a policy advocating one child. To this day, couples "pledging" to have only one child receive a package of benefits from the government.

The national policy sets out the following guidelines: in urban areas, the rewards allocated to couples who sign the one-child certificate include monthly cash payments for 14 years and preference in housing allocation and job assignments; single children receive priority in free medical care and schooling, and jobs at graduation. According to the original policy, rural couples pledging to have one child were promised extra work points (the "currency" earned by farmers working communal land that determined their share of a commune's income) for 14 years, generous allocations of private land and larger grain rations.

Couples that don't comply, and give birth to a third child, have their salaries reduced for the 14-year period, don't receive additional housing space, and have to bear the full costs of that child's birth, medical care and schooling.

National Policy

The Chinese have built the world's most comprehensive family planning network, one that operates on the same principle of decentralization that made the barefoot doctor famous the world over. At its best, the network has been the prime conduit for educating millions of Chinese on the economic, environmental, and health benefits of family planning. At its worst, it has become a tool of coercion.

One result of the Chinese commitment to family planning is that more than 73 percent of couples of reproductive age use a modern form of contraception, a rate that exceeds even the United States' at 68 percent. Moreover, the Chinese populace is highly educated about the benefits to maternal and infant health derived from lower fertility, birth-spacing, and contraceptive use.

In fact, the level of education among Chinese people about one subject, the impact of population on natural resources, probably is higher than anywhere else in the world. The national government suggests but does not dictate the actual package of incentives and disincentives; national policy is interpreted and carried out by planned-birth committees in every province, prefecture, municipality, county and township. Among other things, these committees, made up largely of female cadres, midwives, and other family planning workers, visit households to

120

distribute contraceptives and urge couples to comply with family planning policy.

Decentralization has had its down side, however. Because policies become increasingly more specific as they move down the chain of command, cadres have much more power than is immediately apparent. It is the mandate of local leaders to meet regional and provincial population-size and growth-rate targets. The pressure to do so has, in some provinces, resulted in incidents of coercion, including forced abortions and the mandatory insertion of an intrauterine device following a woman's first live birth, as well as criminal penalties for its removal.

Resistance on the Farm

The one-child policy raises important questions about equity, individual choice, and human rights. To date, many more urban than rural couples have signed on to the one-child policy, accentuating a difference between urban and rural fertility in China similar to that found in most developing countries.

In rural areas, where human labor is still the key ingredient in food production and rural industries, a family's success depends on the number of children it has to tend the fields — even more so now that agricultural reforms have largely privatized Chinese agriculture. It's in peasant homes, where sons are required to support their parents in old age, that the one-child policy faces the most resistance.

Unlike daughters (who generally live with and contribute to the household economy of their in-laws), Chinese sons are bound by tradition and social mores to care for their own parents. Most rural dwellers are not covered by a state-funded pension system. While rural townships are legally bound to provide the "five guarantees" (food, shelter, clothing, medical care and burial) to elderly couples without a son, studies have shown that, even in well-off areas, this program provides minimal aid at best.

Small Happiness

In Chinese, the phrase describing a pregnant woman translates roughly into English as "she has happiness". When a woman gives birth to a son, she has "big happiness"; a daughter brings her "small happiness". Making the birth of a girl equally as welcome as that of a boy is a key challenge to improving human rights and equity, not only in China, but throughout most of the world.

Raising the status of women is a goal in itself. The near-universal discrimination suffered by women in virtually every sphere of their lives has curtailed their social, economic and personal development, severely impaired their health, and deprived them of self-esteem and fulfillment. Measured in terms of education and income levels, women's status also bears on fertility. The more opportunities women have, the fewer children they are likely to bear.

A distinctive preference for sons among a large sector of the Chinese population remains one of the biggest roadblocks to acceptance of the one-child family. About 60 percent of all one-child certificate holders have a son, a fact that has disturbing implications for the status of women and equity in general. In some parts of the country, where women are caught between the demands of the state to limit fertility and the demands of the husband's family to bear a son, violence against both mothers and first-born daughters has increased.

Production vs. Reproduction

The one-child policy cannot be divorced from another campaign going on in China. The "four modernizations", as the name implies, is a drive to increase per-capita production and investment in four key areas — agriculture, industry, defense, and science and technology. The Chinese government, says Qian Xinzhong, minister of public health until 1983, is worried that if population growth continues at its current pace "we will be compelled to devote a considerable amount of. . .resources to feeding the newly increased populace. That will inevitably slow down the four modernizations."

The modernization of agriculture has taken the form of the widely publicized "agricultural responsibility" system, wherein communes and work brigades have given way to the family farm. Under the responsibility system, a family's success depends on its labor resources. This has created an ironic clash between agricultural and family planning policy. In some areas, plots of land are allocated according to the number of laborers a family has, a direct conflict with the disincentives not having more than one child.

Holding the Line

Recent changes notwithstanding, the future of the one-child family program may hinge on the government's willingness to address mounting concerns over social security and inequity. As recent events in Tiananmen Square indicate, a nascent democratic movement exists in China, and the country may be on the brink of a political as well as an economic transition. If this happens, a vocal and organized opposition could develop; indeed, this may eventually happen even in the absence of government reform. A backlash to family planning in China, similar to the one that occurred in India in the mid-seventies in response to forced sterilizations, is conceivable.

With the one-child family, the Chinese have had to chart an unmapped course in the murky waters of human reproductive behavior. The positive aspects of their family planning efforts are evident: lower fertility, better health, and reduced pressure on natural resources and the economy.

But the one-child policy raises a fundamental conflict, one that more and more countries are now facing: the rights of this generation to reproduce against those of future generations to an ecologically intact world.

18 POPULATION CONTROL AND SOCIAL JUSTICE

CHINA'S ONE-CHILD POLICY: Points And Counterpoints

Sara Engram vs. Julian L. Simon

Sara Engram wrote her editorial for the Baltimore Evening Sun. *Julian Simon teaches business administration at the University of Maryland and traveled to China in 1987.*

Points to Consider:

1. What is China's "unemployment problem"?

2. Why does Sara Engram feel that China's policy is a good one? Explain.

3. How is coercion used to enforce the one-child policy?

4. Why does Julian Simon believe we should not support such policies? Explain your answer.

Sara Engram, "Family Planning in China Deserves World Support", **The Baltimore Evening Sun,** February 28, 1988, and Julian L. Simon, "China's Voluntary Population Initiative", **The Wall Street Journal,** February 29, 1988. Reprinted with permission of the **Wall Street Journal.** © 1988 Dow Jones & Company, Inc. All rights reserved.

THE POINT — Sara Engram

By the turn of the century, China will need to find new jobs for about 50 percent of its rural population, which now numbers more than 800 million people. That's an unemployment problem of more than 400 million people—almost twice the entire population of the United States.

To the rest of the world China has always stood apart, a source of civilization and culture long before the West developed. We know it now as an impoverished land determined to put its vast population to work in the campaign to modernize an ancient, tradition-born culture. But even though China has long held a fascination for Westerners, outsiders are still overwhelmed by the size of the challenge facing this country, a challenge complicated by the sheer numbers of people involved. It's typical of human behavior that we tend instead to see Chinese problems through the lens of our own culture.

That habit helps account for the uproar in the United States about China's family-planning program, an ambitious effort begun early in the 1980s with the goal of limiting the country's population—already the world's largest—to 1.2 billion in the year 2000 and a mere 1.5 billion by 2050. To do so, the country must keep its birthrate below 1.5 percent.

In many developing countries family planning programs play a crucial role in helping women space their children far enough apart to give them a decent chance to survive. In more prosperous countries, family planning gives couples control over some of the most important decisions of their lives.

But in China, family planning has become a matter of national survival. The government has faced up to an unpleasant but very real fact: China's birthrate is a time bomb that will either be defused by a disciplined population-control program, or explode to proportions utterly beyond the capacity of the land and its resources to support.

That's a projection that should worry the rest of the world as well. Instead, the U.S. responded with harsh criticisms of China's one-child policy, using reports of coerced abortions as its excuse for denying U.S. funding to the United Nations Fund for Population Activities and as a reason for withdrawing support from other international family planning programs. There are no indications that the Chinese government will back off from its policy. Yet there is plenty of reason to doubt that it will succeed in meeting its population goal.

In 1987, for the second straight year, the country exceeded its birthrate targets. If continued, the year's birthrate of two percent would bring China's population to two billion by 2030. To put meaning to those numbers, consider how many millions of people would be added to that "unemployment problem" China is already coping with, how much more food will be needed to avoid the famines that have plagued the country throughout its history, and how much more housing will be needed simply to keep up with population growth (never mind any efforts to ease the overcrowding that already is a fact of life).

When the new figures were announced in 1988, Wang Wei, the family-planning minister who has enforced the policy with more moderation than his predecessor, was fired.

In the cities, crowded housing conditions help curb the demand for more children, but in the countryside, where economic reforms are allowing peasant families to earn more money, growing numbers of rural Chinese are able to afford the fines imposed for extra children. And since more children mean more labor, there is a built-in incentive for many of these families to ignore the government policy.

Clearly, China's economic and family-planning policies are sending mixed messages to peasant families. But that conflict doesn't change the dire predictions for China's future. Neither do the qualms of outsiders. Almost every culture takes delight in children, but it is hard to watch Chinese families doting over their one, precious child and not admit that these people are making an enormous sacrifice—for the greater good of their country and, ultimately, for the stability of the rest of the world.

We Americans aren't even willing to raise enough taxes to pay our debts. Yet we take on the role of moral policemen for people who are trying to prevent global tragedy a few decades down the road. What's so moral about that?

THE COUNTERPOINT—Julian Simon

Beijing's announcement that it will use stricter means to implement its "one-couple-one-child" policy—including punishments for party cadres and individual families who don't fall in with national goals—has once again put its population program in the headlines.

Planned Parenthood and the rest of the population establishment assert that the Chinese program is voluntary. They should think again. To the Chinese, the word "voluntary" includes pressuring someone until she or he agrees to use contraception or abortion. In the U.S. we call that arm-twisting.

This is supported by official Chinese sources. Indeed, although Chinese authorities repudiate particular events—such as coerced seven-month abortions—as unrepresentative excesses, the presence of government coercion in Chinese family affairs cannot be denied. Consider, for example, the "Eight Visits" of the family planning program in Hengdong County of Hunan province, as described in a Peking University professional journal:

"The 'eight visits' are paid constantly and regularly. . . .

1. The visit is paid to youths at marriageable age for heart-to-heart talks persuading them of late marriage.

2. The visit is paid to newlyweds who are greeted with congratulations and who are mobilized for late childbearing . . .visited by cadres. . .to know their life after marriage, to introduce the knowledge about contraception, to examine their contraceptive measures and to persuade their practice of late childbearing.

3. The visit is made to single child families to mobilize the couples to get single child certificates.

4-6. Visit four is made to persuade married women 'by thorough and painstaking ideological work,' of birth control. Visits five and six are made after sterilization to one-child families.

7-8. Visit seven 'is paid to the employees who are on home leave for family reunion, and they are reminded of contraception.' And visit eight is to "old folks to show care-taking for them. . . ."

The difference between American and Chinese notions of what is voluntary stems from different views about the proper role of government in people's management of their own lives. The Chinese family-planning theorists make much of the comments of Marx concerning the "production" of human beings. A member of China's Family Planning Commission interprets Marx as follows:

"Social production is composed of material production and human reproduction. . . .The socialist system in China [emphasizes both] material production and human reproduction, and [must] regulate population growth in a planned way, as we regulate material production following plans."

Thus the Chinese have complained about U.S. value judgments of their program. Xu Dixin, the chairman of the China Population Society, wrote: "Recently some Americans advertised that since population would automatically decrease with the development of free economy, there was no need to 'limit births'. . . .They have proposed undisguisedly that China's population problem can be settled only by changing her social system and practicing 'free economy'. Such arguments made by some Americans are presumptuous to interfere politically in China's internal affairs and to sabotage her socialist system."

Refraining from comment, however, does not imply that one should help. Nations have no obligation to fund programs of which they do not approve. Even the touchy Chinese must agree that this is not "internal interference".

In this regard the world could follow the U.S. lead in shifting money away from organizations, such as the United Nations Fund for Population Activities, found to support or participate in coercive programs. Countries that want to use their population funds to further China's development would do well to train more Chinese demographers in the West. Perhaps this might include giving them a firsthand look at Asia's own models of development under freedom, notably Hong Kong and Taiwan. What could be simpler, purer of heart, possibly doing some good and certainly avoiding harm?

19   POPULATION CONTROL AND SOCIAL JUSTICE

POPULATION CONTROL AS A WOMEN'S HEALTH ISSUE

Adrienne Germain and Jane Ordway

Adrienne Germain and Jane Ordway prepared this report on population control for the International Women's Health Coalition (IWHC) in cooperation with the Overseas Development Council. The IWHC seeks to improve reproductive health and dignity for girls and women throughout the Third World.

Points to Consider:

1. Why is population more than a problem of contraception?

2. What problems are encountered by Third World women? Why?

3. What do Third World women want?

4. Why must contraceptives be made more available to women in the developing nations?

Adrienne Germain and Jane Ordway, "Population Control and Women's Health: Balancing the Scales", published by the International Women's Health Coalition, June 1989.

Solving the "population problem" requires more than simply provision of contraceptives.

To most people, the "population problem" means "overpopulation", primarily in the Third World, where three-quarters of the world's five billion people live. "Overpopulation" conjures up images of malnourished and dying children, burgeoning slums, deforestation and desertification, and an unending cycle of poverty, disease, illiteracy, and social and political chaos. Population growth, along with poorly planned industrialization and environmental destruction, are seen as threats to sustaining life at acceptable levels in the future.

Hoping to change this devastating prospect, family planning and related programs have supplied millions of women in the Third World with contraceptives which would otherwise be unavailable to them. Most such programs have viewed women as producers of too many babies and as potential contraceptive "acceptors". The tendency to neglect other aspects of women's reproductive health has often undermined or negated the achievement of effective and widespread contraceptive use, however. For example, inappropriate contraceptive use due to poor counseling, and high discontinuation rates due to side effects or infection, among other causes, are common in the Third World.

The "population problem" and possible solutions need careful review and redefinition. A "reproductive health" approach, with women at its center, could considerably strengthen the achievements of existing family planning and health programs, while helping women to attain health, dignity, and basic rights.

The Population Problem

Solving the "population problem" requires more than simply provision of contraceptives. Fertility control involves the most intimate of human relations, complex behaviors, and substantial risks. To control their own reproduction, therefore, women must also be able to achieve social status and dignity, to manage their own health and sexuality, and to exercise their basic rights in society and in partnerships with men.

Early sexual relations and pregnancy, however, curtail education, employment, and other social and political opportunities for millions of young women in the Third World, just as they do for one million teenage women in the United States every year. Prevention of adolescent pregnancy will require social acceptance of sex education and contraceptive

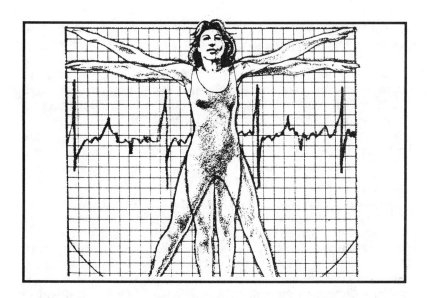

services for teens, wide-ranging support for development of young women's self-esteem, and other interventions that are politically or otherwise challenging.

Third World women who become pregnant face a risk of death due to pregnancy that is 50 to 200 times higher than that of women in industrial countries. Pregnant adolescents frequently face obstructed labor that culminates in death or serious physical damage. Sixty percent of pregnant women in the Third World are anemic, which makes them especially vulnerable to problems in pregnancy and labor that result in death. Over half, in some countries 80-90 percent, of pregnant women give birth without trained assistance or emergency care. As many as 250-375,000 women are estimated to die annually when giving birth. This tragedy is intensified manyfold by its impacts on the families left behind.

Fears about the safety of modern contraceptives are strong deterrents to contraceptive use. Women must bear most of the social and health risks of modern contraception, partly because contraceptive methods available to men are extremely limited in number and appeal. Condoms have no side effects and can be very useful in preventing spread of disease, but men are often reluctant to use them and women are not in a position to persuade them to. Similarly, vasectomy, safer and simpler than female sterilization, is practiced far less in the Third World. Thus, population control requires development of new and improved contraceptive methods.

Increasingly, women in the Third World who do not want to be pregnant avoid pregnancy by using contraception effectively. But millions of women have unwanted pregnancies. Many of these carry their pregnancies to term and end up with one to three more children than they want. Every year an estimated 30-45 million pregnant Third World women who cannot accept a birth resort to abortion. And every year, at least 125,000 of them—and quite possibly at least twice that many—die in the process. Uncounted others are rendered sterile or suffer severe chronic health consequences. Those who survive abortion often face greatly increased risk of death in subsequent pregnancies.

Sexuality and sexual relationships are fraught with other dangers for girls and women that also affect their view about fertility and contraception. First, millions suffer sexually transmitted diseases (STDs), including AIDS, transmitted by men. As a result of STDs, botched abortion, harmful surgical practices, or their partners' infertility, among other causes, millions of women are subfertile or infertile. They live in dread of divorce and social ostracism because they cannot bear children. Second, millions are subject to violence due to their gender—rape, incest, and emotional and physical battering by husbands or relatives.

Third World Needs

Women want to be healthy, and to have as many children as they want, when they want them, without risk to their own or their children's health. They want services for their own health, for safe delivery of healthy infants and for child health. They want means to space or to limit their childbearing that are easily available.

Many women now excluded as a matter of policy from contraceptive services want access. In many countries, these include the young, the unmarried, and those who do not yet have a child. Many women need easier access to services.

Women determined to avoid birth want safe services for terminating an unwanted pregnancy. Unlike women in most Western countries and in China, most Third World women face highly restricted access to such services due to legal restrictions or failure to make services available, even where legal, as in India.

Women want to be treated with respect. They want full information, supportive counseling, the choice to terminate pregnancy safely, choices among contraceptive methods, and follow-up care to cope with side effects or to enable them to

WHAT IS REPRODUCTIVE HEALTH CARE?

It is comprehensive, providing:

- *Education on sexuality and hygiene;*
- *Education, screening and treatment for reproductive tract infections, and gynecological problems resulting from sexuality, age, multiple births and birth trauma;*
- *Counseling about sexuality, contraception, abortion, infertility, infection and disease;*
- *Infertility prevention and treatment;*
- *Choices among contraceptive methods, with systematic attention to contraceptive safety;*
- *Safe menstrual regulation and abortion for contraceptive failure or non-use;*
- *Prenatal care, supervised delivery and post-partum care;*
- *Infant and child health services.*

It is high quality:

- *Treating clients with respect and compassion;*
- *Following them up.*

It is premised on informed choice:

- *Providing full information;*
- *Encouraging continued use of services, rather than just initial acceptance.*

Adrienne Germain and Jane Ordway, "Population Control and Women's Health: Balancing the Scales", published by the International Women's Health Coalition, June 1989

switch contraceptive methods.

Women also want services to meet their multiple reproductive health needs. Millions of Third World women face the discomforts and consequences of reproductive tract infections, including the personal and social trauma of infertility. Little or no counseling or treatment is available to women suffering from infertility or sexually transmitted diseases, often a consequence of their partners' sexual behavior rather than of their own.

More and better contraceptives, for both men and women, must be developed, along with programs to enable women (and men) to undertake sexual relations safely.

The Challenge Ahead

Virtually nowhere in the Third World are contraceptives available to all the women—and men—who want them. Some argue, therefore, that programmatic priority should continue to emphasize contraceptive supply and acceptance. It is not enough simply to make commodities available, however. To serve women well, and to reduce attacks from both the Right and the Left, contraceptives must be made available in settings where quality of services, counseling, choices among methods, and respect for reproductive freedom are prominent.

At the urging of women's health advocates and others, population professionals now recognize that the earlier focus on contraceptive acceptance rates needs to be broadened. Women in the Third World are calling for more comprehensive services that provide them with reproductive choices and that reduce ill health and death resulting from their sexual and reproductive roles. The central objectives of "reproductive health" programming are therefore to enable Third World women to:

- Regulate their own fertility safely and effectively by conceiving when desired, by terminating unwanted pregnancies, and by carrying wanted pregnancies to term;

- Remain free of disease, disability, or danger of death due to reproduction and sexuality;

- Bear and raise healthy children.

"Population" is a fundamentally human problem. The solutions must be both humane and responsive to the complexities of people's behavior. For both humanitarian and political reasons, those concerned about population growth need also to reaffirm their commitment to individual well-being. That commitment can be enacted by making reproductive choices possible, by modifying program approaches to emphasize quality of care, and by recognizing and seeking to meet women's multiple reproductive health needs. The potential scope for innovation is broad. In setting program priorities, it is essential to recognize that the woman is important in her own right, as well as the key actor in fertility regulation and in infant and child health. Her needs, not just those of her children, family, and society, must be central. Alliances for this purpose will be to the benefit of all.

20   POPULATION CONTROL AND SOCIAL JUSTICE

POPULATION CONTROL AS A POLITICAL ISSUE

David C. Huff

David Huff is the chief financial officer of Fox-Rowden-McBrayer in Atlanta, Georgia.

Points to Consider:

1. How does the author view the family?

2. Why do governments consider children as property?

3. What is the "propaganda explosion"? Explain.

David C. Huff, "Freedom, Coercion, and Family Size", **The Freeman,** January 1989.

Population control is an uncannily accurate objective for a movement whose prime motivation is, indeed, control.

The freedom of a husband and wife to bear as many children as they wish is an implicit aspect of the principles of liberty upon which our nation was founded. America's early citizens and statesmen clearly understood the many social and economic advantages of large families, recognizing in the family structure a rich treasure of ingredients for the sustenance of society which far overshadows any benefits a civil government can provide. As Gary North has observed:

"The family. . .provides a basic division of labor, and this leads to greater productivity. It provides a zone of safety against life's battles with a fallen, recalcitrant environment. . . .It provides men and women with a stake in the future, and in so doing, makes possible habits of thrift that lead to vast capital growth . . . .It provides welfare and education for its members. It reduces the need for a huge state bureaucracy, so it acts as a weapon against the illegitimate expansion of state power."

The Cornerstone

As might be expected, the concept of the family as the cornerstone of a free society, a principal steward of a society's capital, and a key facet (through steady population increase) of a society's economic vitality has not lacked detractors. Most parents with more than two children would agree that large families are subtly and sometimes noisily discouraged today. The task for advocates of freedom is to inquire beyond the specific bias against large families and discern the root ideology involved. It will prove to be quite familiar.

Any consideration of the freedoms involved in choosing family size necessarily involves the larger issue of ownership and property rights. Even to question the fact that the ownership and responsibility for children vests exclusively in their parents once would have seemed superfluous. Yet in the current environment of Zero Population Growth, Planned Parenthood, and Global 2000, private ownership of children no longer enjoys unanimous consent: "The 'right' to breed implies ownership of children. This concept is no longer tenable. Society pays an even larger share of the cost of raising and educating children. The idea of ownership is surely affected by the thrust of the saying that 'He who pays the piper calls the tune'."

136

Does this tune sound familiar? While one obvious response is the insight that a "society" has no existence or identity apart from the individuals composing it, such a coercive mind-set merely regurgitates a common statist strategy. Any drive for omnipotence by the state or its agents always involves an insatiable appetite to control private property for the "good of society". And understandably so, since the ownership and control of private property is integral to a free society and therefore an inherent enemy of central planning.

Given that the tenets of interventionism idolize the state as a benevolent, all-wise parent to its children, it is not a difficult leap for government to concoct a policy which includes seizure of the "right to breed" and thereby arrogates the ultimate control of family size to the state. Only then can it begin to enact the kind of "necessary" controls (to protect society, of course) envisioned by some: "It can be argued that over-production—that is, the bearing of more than four children—is a worse crime than most and should be outlawed. One thinks of the possibility of raising the minimum age of marriage, of imposing stiff penalties for illegitimate pregnancy, of compulsory sterilization after a fifth birth."

We see, then, that in order for a bureaucracy to gain its desired position of pseudo-parent and thereby the power to control family size, it must begin by usurping property rights over children.

Malthus and Human Capital

As alluded to earlier, the barbs directed at prolific parents generally are launched from the various elements of the population control movement. Their basic message is that our planet is becoming overpopulated, which in turn will purportedly cause food shortages, destroy the balance of nature, wreck economies, and generally drive civilized society into extinction.

This population control ideology had its origins in the theories of Thomas Malthus, who two centuries ago predicted a population crisis which would shackle the world in the perpetual grip of poverty. The passage of time, however, has not seen the fulfillment of his dismal prophecies—but it has yielded decades of experience which show that healthy population growth is an asset, not a threat:

"The basic axiom of economics—both classical and modern—is that wealth is the product of labor. The mineral resources of the earth are not wealth until human effort has been exerted, either to discover or extract them."

137

Throughout the ages—until the current era of statistics-worship—population has been regarded as the foremost source of wealth; the prime object of rulers and governments has been to attract and increase the number of their people. Density of population and rising population historically have been the mark of a prosperous, vital civilization."

By their very nature, Malthusian precepts (which have been substantially disproved) are ideologically at war against the principle of human capital expansion through population increase. This seems strange, when the evidence in favor of large families and growth is amply available.

So again, to fully comprehend the real issue, one must uncover the motivation of those who fret over the "population bomb". Is the issue actually conservation—of resources, living space, and the balance of nature—or is the issue control of the human capital represented?

The Propaganda Explosion

An exhaustive chronicle of the many factors working toward family size limitation by force is beyond the scope of this brief essay. Nevertheless, the fundamental idea which should be retained is the insight that discouragement of large families represents but one narrow symptom of an age-old, chronic illness—interventionism. The dangerous explosion has not been population, but propaganda.

Population control is an uncannily accurate objective for a

movement whose prime motivation is, indeed, control. The march of the state toward attainment of the power of life and death over its citizens, if unchecked, will allow no competing sovereignty on the part of individuals or families. Thus, not only the right to bear children, but the very sanctity of human life must be diligently guarded and defended. For as Frederic Wertham notes, "If someone in authority tells us that we have no right to procreate, it is only one step further for him to tell us we have no right to live."

History bears telling witness to an observation which captures the essence of the family-limiting philosphy: "Population control is the last desperate act and ultimate weapon of a Welfare State whose lust for power and instinct for survival knows no political or moral limits."

21 POPULATION CONTROL AND SOCIAL JUSTICE

POPULATION CONTROL AS AN ECONOMIC ISSUE

Colleen Lowe Morna

Colleen Lowe Morna is a Zimbabwe-based freelance journalist.

Points to Consider:

1. Why is Zimbabwe more agriculturally efficient than its neighbors?

2. How have pricing policies helped Zimbabwe?

3. Describe the new opportunities for women.

4. What marketing methods have benefited Zimbabwe?

Colleen Lowe Morna, "A Maize Miracle", **New Internationalist,** June 1990.

As Africa enters the 1990s, Zimbabwe's agricultural success is attracting increasing attention.

Zimbabwe's communal farmers have offered a beacon of hope for Africa during the 1980s. Elsewhere on the continent most governments have adopted policies skewed against agriculture and in favor of the politically vocal urban elite. Agricultural exports have declined, and food imports are increasing at seven percent a year.

Neighboring Zambia, for example, has perhaps three times the agricultural potential of Zimbabwe. But until recently it imported more food than it exported due to its concentration on copper mining. Zimbabwe became independent in 1980, long after its neighbors, and it learned from their mistakes. It has prioritized agriculture, trying to maintain productivity among the 5,000 largely white commercial farmers and to increase production among the 850,000 peasant families.

Under the former government, communal farmers never delivered more than 80,000 tons to the Grain Marketing Board. That amount has since increased tenfold. Except in a drought year, Zimbabwe's small-scale farmers can now feed the nation, freeing commercial farmers to produce for export.

Stunning Success

This is impressive enough but peasant farmers do not only grow food. Today they also grow 55 percent of Zimbabwe's cotton, 90 percent of its sunflowers and 30 to 40 percent of its groundnuts. Overall agriculture accounts for 45 percent of Zimbabwe's exports, sustains half its industries and is the country's largest single employer.

As Africa enters the 1990s, Zimbabwe's agricultural success is attracting increasing attention. Under Ian Smith's former white minority government, peasant farmers were cramped into the worst land. But the present government aims to buy unproductively used "white" land and settle peasant farmers there. One-third of the 165,000 families originally targeted for resettlement have been moved. With a population growth rate of almost four percent a year, however, resettlement is only one answer to Zimbabwe's problems. "Of course we want land in the most productive areas," says Gapare. "But also training and other forms of support can make unproductive land productive."

Zimbabwe's major departure from its neighbors — and chief incentive to its farmers — has been a consistent pricing policy.

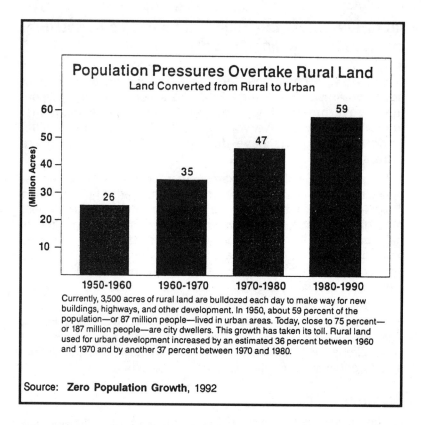

Population Pressures Overtake Rural Land
Land Converted from Rural to Urban

(Million Acres)

- 26 — 1950-1960
- 35 — 1960-1970
- 47 — 1970-1980
- 59 — 1980-1990

Currently, 3,500 acres of rural land are bulldozed each day to make way for new buildings, highways, and other development. In 1950, about 59 percent of the population—or 87 million people—lived in urban areas. Today, close to 75 percent—or 187 million people—are city dwellers. This growth has taken its toll. Rural land used for urban development increased by an estimated 36 percent between 1960 and 1970 and by another 37 percent between 1970 and 1980.

Source: **Zero Population Growth,** 1992

While food subsidies to urban consumers were progressively cut between 1982 and 1984, the price of maize, Zimbabwe's staple food, more than doubled over the same period. The price subsequently remained flat for three years because of a huge stockpile and low prices on the international market. But prices have since been readjusted to about Z$50 (U.S.$25) per ton, which enables farmers to make a decent profit.

Just as important as the pricing policy has been the increase of credit. Under the former government—as in many African countries today—most peasant farmers couldn't borrow money because they didn't have collateral. Now, although most loans still go to commercial farmers, lending to peasant farmers has shot up from Z$250,000 in 1979/80 to the present level of Z$30 million annually.

"The main change," says the general manager of the Agricultural Corporation which controls most loans, "was not to insist on collateral but to give loans on the basis of viability of the program."

Role of Women

There has been another big legal change—to the position of women. In the past women were regarded as minors and could only get credit through their husbands. Today all Zimbabweans become majors at the age of 18 and women can get loans as long as they present a viable project, live on the farm and have a good knowledge of farming.

Mavis Mukwauri is one farmer who has benefited. She, like many African women, does the farming while her husband works in town. He is a freelance painter who can't get work during the rainy season—precisely when she needs money to buy agricultural materials.

In 1986, Mukwauri suggested to her husband that they take out a loan. "He said to me: 'do whatever you can do; you are the farmer'." So she borrowed enough money to buy materials for four acres of land. That season she reaped 96 bags of maize, compared to her previous 20. Over the last two years she has increased her coverage to six acres and now averages 120 bags of maize.

Racial Equity

Improved extension services or backup for peasant farmers have also been vital in Zimbabwe's agricultural revolution. Before independence, such services were split in two along racial lines, with most going to white commercial farmers. Since independence, the services have been amalgamated and their budget tripled to 30 million Zimbabwe dollars, or 20 percent of agriculture's total budget.

The Zimbabwean government has realized that every part of the agricultural process needs improving, from borrowing money right through to transporting the grain to market—a total package. Thus agricultural training facilities have also expanded since 1980: despite the growth in population over the period, the ratio of agricultural demonstrators to farmers has been reduced from 1:1000 to 1:850. And they are making a special effort to target women farmers, who have traditionally been ignored.

"In the old days it was very difficult for me to talk to women farmers, because the men would say 'look, he's trying to steal my wife'," says one agricultural demonstrator. "Now since the government says we are all equal, it is much easier."

One farmer who has learned a lot from the demonstrator is Ebba Chirumanza. "I did not understand the benefits of winter ploughing, or which type of fertilizer to use for my soil, or how to grow cash crops like cotton," she says. And but for the demonstrator, "I would not know how to mix pesticides easily myself because I can't read the labels."

A Better Network

Farmers have also been helped by the improved marketing infrastructure. Elsewhere in Africa a major impediment to commercial farming has been the deterioration of roads and railways due to budget cuts over the decade.

Zimbabwe fortunately inherited a relatively well-developed network, complemented by an efficient Grain Marketing Board. Before independence all of these facilities were geared to serving the country's white farmers. But since 1980, great efforts have been made to re-orient the facilities. Secondary and feeder roads have been built into rural areas. The number of Grain Marketing Board depots has been increased from 43 to 66 — and all the new ones are located in peasant farming districts. Eventually no small farmer will be further than 45 kilometers away from a marketing facility.

But all these efforts mean nothing if the farmers themselves do not take advantage of them. Above the mantelpiece in Dan Mutsoto's lounge a framed certificate with the National Resource Board logo takes pride of place. In fine print the certificate which bears his name makes commendation of "his exemplary activities in water management and viable land husbandry."

That is the secret of this remarkable Zimbabwean peasant farmer's success. For his stony five-acre plot land in the Chikukwa area of southeast Zimbabwe is hardly a farmer's dream. Last year the proceeds from this rough piece of ground fed Mutsoto's whole family of ten and brought in nearly Z$1,500 in profit—almost three times the country's per capita income. "I try to use every inch of land and use it properly," says the middle-aged farmer, flashing a broad grin.

Initially, like most peasant farmers in Zimbabwe, Mutsoto only grew maize. But when he discovered that he could make three times the amount by growing beans, Mutsoto shifted tactics. For the last two seasons he has primarily been growing beans with just enough maize scattered in between to feed his family.

On the other two acres of land Mutsoto is experimenting with coffee, an increasingly popular crop with peasant farmers in the mountainous regions of the country. Before the winter, Mutsoto is setting up his own irrigation scheme for the crop, using water from a mountain stream. And to capitalize on this investment, he has also decided to put in a crop of winter wheat between the coffee bushes.

Meanwhile, on a slope adjoining the farm, Mutsoto has planted 4,000 trees because he has noticed that "my wife is having to go further and further for firewood." Not to waste any opportunity, Mutsoto has also set up beehives among the trees. "Next time you come," says the amiable farmer as he serves out large chunks of maize bread, "there will be honey to go with the meal."

22 POPULATION CONTROL AND SOCIAL JUSTICE

POPULATION CONTROL AS A NATIONAL SECURITY ISSUE

Elizabeth Sobo

Elizabeth Sobo, an independent journalist specializing in research on foreign influence in Africa, writes a regular column on African music for a U.S. West Coast magazine.

Points to Consider:

1. Who was Ben Wattenberg and what population trend was he worried about?

2. Why did poor nations object to attempts by the U.S. and rich nations to limit their population growth?

3. Why did U.S. policy makers want population growth limited in poor nations?

Excerpted from an article written by Elizabeth Sobo for the **National Catholic Reporter**, November 23, 1990.

General skepticism of U.S.-backed population control remains strong in Africa and elsewhere in the developing world-and there is much to suggest such concerns are legitimate.

A report on sub-Sahara Africa by the World Bank published in 1989 found the continent's "land and water resources are vast. Agriculture production, with the right technology, could be greatly expanded. The considerable mineral potential has yet to be tapped. Africa has massive energy resources in gas reserves and hydropower potential." The study concludes that, "with sound practices and technological innovations, Africa might eventually accommodate several times its present population."

Advocates

Some population-control advocates concede that the wealth, not the poverty, of Africa justifies population control. In his 1987 book, *The Birth Dearth*, American Enterprise Institute scholar Ben Wattenberg warned that low birthrates in the West compounded by high fertility in the developing world will bring about a decline in U.S. cultural and economic influence in the world. The shift in demographic power, he wrote, will mean "Third World nations will also likely be richer and more powerful than they are now."

Thus, wrote Wattenberg, "it is our best long-term interest that fertility rates in the less developed countries come down even more rapidly than they are now falling. . . .We ought to have the courage to say publicly what is true about demographics and not be afraid of being called 'racist' or 'colonial'."

Public discourse on population almost always portrays the impact of high fertility in terms of environmental problems, food shortages and global overcrowding. But those who have shaped U.S. foreign policy hold views similar to Wattenberg's. Population control has historically had its roots in a militaristic view of the world that sees a shrinking West increasingly outnumbered by people of developing countries.

Population Control

The idea of population control in foreign-assistance policy dates to late 1945, when a Gallup Poll asked respondents whether they favored U.S. sponsorship of birth control "education" for World War II enemies Germany and Japan. By a small margin, they did.

More than a decade later, "overpopulation" was given official recognition as a national security issue by a special Committee to Study the United States Military Assistance Program, created in 1959 by Gen. William Draper. And a 1963 report by the Committee to Strengthen the Security of the Free World, headed by Gen. Lucius D. Clay, emphasized the need for economic aid — both for "the curtailment of communist efforts" and to address the potential for "social unrest" posed by "the rapidity of population growth in many areas."

President Eisenhower and John F. Kennedy largely ignored the recommendations for greater involvement from these prestigious panels. Eisenhower strongly supported the idea of private sector population projects, and he later held an honorary position with Planned Parenthood. But he never committed foreign assistance funds for population activities. Kennedy openly opposed such measures on the grounds they might "appear to advocate limitation of the black or brown or yellow peoples whose population is increasing no faster than in the United States."

The Debate

During the early 1960s, the debate was relegated to boardrooms of a dozen population control advocacy groups and foundations, several of which had already begun privately sponsored population programs abroad as well as public relations campaigns at home.

Then came a time of unprecedented change. Racial tensions and wholesale resistance to the war in Vietnam tore the nation internally, while colonial empires in Africa and elsewhere were being dismantled with astonishing speed. Ultimately, the United States was faced with a decline in the power and prestige it had enjoyed since the end of World War II. Perhaps most important to long-range planners in a world where political clout is increasingly swayed by demographics was that birthrates in the United States and Western Europe had begun a sharp and probably irreversible decline.

President Lyndon Johnson was the first to explicitly endorse government-sponsored family planning overseas, setting in place a formula of gradual escalation in population assistance designed largely to minimize criticism within his administration. His public remarks suggest he viewed population control mainly as a means to increase the clout of the foreign aid budget. "Let us act on the fact that less than $5 invested in population control is worth $100 invested in economic growth," he said in a

June 1965 speech commemorating the United Nations' 20th anniversary.

A total of $10.5 million was allocated for international family planning from 1965 to 1967, at which time Congress incorporated funding for population control into the Foreign Assistance Act. The same year, the U.S. Population Fund was created as a trust, largely on the initiative of the U.S. population establishment.

And a year later, population control was incorporated into the World Bank's development strategy with the appointment of Vietnam War-era Defense Secretary Robert McNamara as its president. Another Vietnam War wager, Gen. William Westmoreland, now sits on the board of directors of the Population Crisis Committee in Washington, D.C., a lobbying group Gen. Draper founded in 1965.

President Richard Nixon formally elevated the population control program to "a top priority item" in a then-classified 1970 National Security Council decision memorandum on "The New U.S. Foreign Assistance Program". And his successor, President Gerald Ford, called the "rapid growth of the human race. . .one of the greatest challenges to man's ingenuity that we have ever encountered."

Recipient nations, preoccupied with building their economies and initially disinterested in modern birth control, grew increasingly hostile as the heat was turned up by U.S.-sponsored population reduction operations.

Strong Objections

Strong objections to a U.S.-backed World Population Plan of Action were raised during a 1974 international population conference in Bucharest. Representatives of newly independent African nations, led by Algeria, attacked the proposal on grounds that the problems attributed to overpopulation were the result of economic exploitation and a world economic order that favored wealthy, industrialized countries.

Several Latin American nations, particularly Brazil, Argentina, Uruguay and Peru, protested population control for ethical reasons; and all of Eastern Europe, with the exception of Romania, joined in, calling population control "imperialistic" and "neocolonialist". Most argue that rapid population growth is necessary for development and that birthrates in developing countries would decline after development in much the same way they had done in the United States.

Such resistance to a "top priority item" on Nixon's agenda was not to be taken lightly. Secretary of State Henry Kissinger sent a classified memorandum April 24, 1974, to the secretaries of defense and agriculture, the director of central intelligence, the deputy secretary of state and the AID administrator.

That memo requested a joint study of the "impact of world population growth on U.S. security and overseas interests," including "problems the U.S. may face arising from competition for resources." The study should focus, Kissinger added, "on the international political and economic implications of population growth rather than its ecological, sociological or other aspects."

The resulting study—presented December 10, 1974, four months after Nixon resigned—was formally accepted as official government policy in a National Security Council directive a year later. The study warned of a potential shift in the balance of power as some larger nations increased their proportion of the world's people—predicting, for example, a "growing power status for Brazil in Latin America and on the world scene over the next 25 years" and a "growing political and strategic role for Nigeria."

It pointed also to possible "revolutionary actions" that could result in "expropriation of foreign interests" and the potential growth of left-wing movements bent on attacking multinational corporations and Western influence. U.S. military and industrial needs, it added, "will require large and increasing amounts of minerals from abroad, especially from less developed countries. That fact gives the U.S. enhanced interest in the political, economic and social stability of the supplying countries."

Expanded Assistance

The study recommended that the intelligence capabilities of embassies be enlisted to seize "opportunities for expanding our assistance" and proposed that the United States condition foreign aid on population control performance, consider the possibility of "food rationing" for countries unwilling to slash birthrates and embark upon massive media campaigns to "motivate" people to limit family size.

INTERPRETING EDITORIAL CARTOONS

This activity may be used as individualized study guide for students in libraries and resource centers or as a discussion catalyst in small group and classroom discussions.

Although cartoons are usually humorous, the main intent of most political cartoonists is not to entertain. Cartoons express serious social comment about important issues. Using graphic and visual arts, the cartoonist expresses opinions and attitudes. By employing an entertaining and often light-hearted visual format, cartoonists may have as much or more impact on national and world issues as editorial and syndicated columnists.

Points to Consider:

1. Examine the cartoons on page 82 and 100.

2. How would you describe the message of each cartoon?

3. Try to summarize the messages in one to three sentences.

4. Do the cartoons' messages support the author's point of view in any of the opinions in Chapter Five of this publication? If the answer is yes, be specific about which reading or readings and why.

BIBLIOGRAPHY

Global Population Crisis

Berreby, D. The numbers game. *Discover*, v. 11, April 1990: p. 42-3.

Boyce, J. K. The bomb is a dud. *The Progressive,* v. 54, Sept. 1990: p. 24.

Eberstadt, N. Population change and national security. *Foreign Affairs,* v. 70, Summer 1991: p. 115-131.

Ehrlich, P. R. and Ehrlich, A. H. The population explosion. Simon and Schuster, New York, 1990: 320 p.

Fornos, W. Population Politics. *Technology Review.* v. 94, Feb./Mar. 1991: p. 61-4.

Fox, R. W. Can Central America cope with soaring population? *USA Today* (periodical), v. 120, Sept. 1991: p. 48-52.

The global village. *Utne Reader*, July/August 1990: p. 144.

Hair, J.D. Confronting a controversial subject. *International Wildlife*, v. 21, July/August 1991: p. 26.

Hardin, G. Population. *Buzzworm*, v. 3, Jan./Feb. 1991: p. 35.

Hardy, E. The anti-Malthus views. *Forbes*, v. 146, Dec. 10, 1990: p. 110+.

Henry, W. A. Beyond the melting pot. *Time,* v. 135, April 9, 1990: p. 28-31.

Koretz, G. Yesterday's 'birth dearth': tomorrow's housing bust? *Business Week,* Dec. 30, 1991: p. 26.

Malthus, T. R. Population: the first essay. *University of Michigan Press,* 1959: 139 p.

Miller, J. Reinventing the brake: Report from the Philippines. *Commonweal,* Feb. 24, 1989: p. 105-7.

Misch, A. Purdah and overpopulation in the Middle East. *Worldwatch*, Nov./Dec. 1990: p. 10-11.

Morain, M. Population update. *The Humanist,* v. 50, July/Aug. 1990: p. 37.

Nielsen, J. What ever happened to the population bomb? *National Wildlife,* v. 28, April/May 1990: p. 28.

Peterson, W. Malthus: the reactionary reformer. *The American Scholar*, v. 59, Spring 1990: p. 275-82.

Rubenstein, E. The more the merrier. *National Review,* v. 42, Dec. 17, 1990: p. 14.

Sadik, N. World population continues to rise. *The Futurist,* v. 25, March/April 1991: p. 9-14.

Sadik, N. World population growth unchecked. *USA Today* (periodical), v. 120, August 1991: p. 10.

Shiva, V. The rest of reality [India]. *Ms.* v. 1, Nov./Dec. 1990: p. 72-73.

Simon, J. L. The ultimate resource. *Princeton University Press,* 1981: 415 p.

Sudan: the 'silent dying'. *Newsweek,* April 15, 1991: p. 46.

Tierney, J. A bet on planet Earth. *Reader's Digest,* v. 138, March 1991.

World population growth rate slows. *The Futurist,* v. 24, May/June 1990: p. 56.

Environment

Brown, L. R. State of the world—1991. *Worldwatch Institute,* W. W. Norton, 1991: 253 p.

Ehrlich, P. R. and Ehrlich, A. H. Growing, growing, gone. *Sierra,* v. 75, March/April 1990: p. 36-40.

Gergen, D. Collisions ahead for environmentalists. *U.S. News & World Report,* v. 108, May 7, 1990: p.37.

Lawton, K. A. Is there room for pro-life environmentalists? *Christianity Today,* v. 34, Sept 24, 1990: p. 46-47.

Simon, J. L. People, resources, environment and immigration. Transaction Publishers, New Brunswick, U.S.A. and London, U.K., 1990.

Food and Biotechnology

Avery, D. Global food progress 1991. *Hudson Institute,* 1991.

Coping with famine. *Time,* v. 137, June 10, 1991: p. 28.

Crawford, R. Gene mapping Japan's number one crop. *Science,* v. 252, June 21, 1991: p. 1611.

Crawley, M. J. Sixty thousand seeds sown by hand. *Bio Science,* v. 41, April 1991: p. 208.

Harris-Monin, F. Plants for the future. *World Press Review,* v. 37, October 1990: p. 64.

Linden, E. Will we run low on food? *Time,* v. 138, Aug. 19, 1991: p. 48-50.

Population Control and Abortion

Asia: discarding daughters. *Time,* v. 136, Fall 1990: p. 40.

Byrne, H. J. A house divided: the pro-life movement. *America,* v. 164, Jan. 5-12, 1991: p. 6-10.

A case for family planning? *Christianity Today,* v. 35, June 24, 1991: p. 49.

Christensen, J. In Brazil, sterilizing women is the method of choice. *Progressive,* Sept. 1990: p. 22-28.

Conner, R. Demographic doomsayers. *Current,* v. 320, Feb. 1990: p. 21-25.

Donaldson, P. J. and Tsui, A. O. Family planning in the third world. *The Futurist,* v. 25, May/June 1991: p. 51-52.

Is birth control Christian? *Christianity Today,* v. 35, Nov. 11, 1991: p. 34-45.

Jacobson, J. The global aspects of abortion. *Utne Reader,* March/April 1991: p. 55-59.

Kaplan, D. A. Abortion: Just say no advice. *Newsweek,* v. 117, June 3, 1991: p. 18.

McCulloch, H. L. Abortion cut-off. *Nation,* v. 250, April 9, 1990: p. 477.

McGowan, J. You can't have too many kids. *U.S. Catholic,* v. 56, March 1991: p. 34-36.

Ozanne, J. Kenya fights its baby boom. *World Press Review,* v. 37, July 1990: p. 67.

Population Technical Assistance Project (U.S.A.I.D.). Mexico City policy implementation study. November 1990.

Willimon, W. H. A uniquely Christian stand on abortion. *The Christian Century,* v. 108, Feb. 27, 1991: p. 220-221.

China

Aird, J. S. Slaughter of the innocents: Coercive birth control in China. Washington, American Enterprise Institute for Public Policy Research, 1990.

Banister, J. China's population changes and the economy. U.S. Congress, Joint Economic Committee, April 1991.

China's population growth could lower standard of living. *Society,* v. 28, Nov./Dec. 1990: p. 2-3.

Chua, J. 'Unstudly.' *The New Republic,* v. 206, Jan. 27, 1992: p. 11.

Coale, A. J. Recent trends in fertility in China. *Science,* v. 251, Jan. 25, 1991: p. 389-93.

Delfs, R. China's fertility factor. *World Press Review*, v. 37, Nov. 1990: p. 71.

McGowan, J. Little girls dying. *Commonweal,* v. 118, Aug. 9, 1991: p. 481-2.

Smil, V. Feeding China's people. *Current History*, v. 89, Sept. 1990: p. 257-60.

White, T. China's one-child policy. U.S. Congress, Joint Economic Committee, April 1991.

Appendix

POPULATION RESOURCE LIST

For further information on issues of global population, write to the following organizations:

NON-GOVERNMENTAL

Alan Guttmacher Institute (AGI)
111 5th Avenue
New York, NY 10003 USA

American Public Health Association
1015 15th St. NW, 3rd Floor
Washington, D.C. 20005 USA

Asia Foundation
P.O. Box 3223
San Francisco, CA 94119-3223 USA

Bread for the World
802 Rhode Island Ave. NE
Washington, D.C. 20018 USA

Center for Population Options (CPO)
1025 Vermont Av. NW, Suite 210
Washington, DC 20005 USA

Environmental Fund
1325 G Street NW, Suite 1003
Washington, D.C. 20005 USA

International Council on Management of Population Programmes
141 Jalan Dahlia
Taman Uda Jaya
68000 Ampang,
Kuala Lumpur, Malaysia

International Planned Parenthood Federation (IPPF)
18-20 Lower Regent Street
London SW1 4PW, England

International Women's Health Coalition (IWHC)
24 E. 21st Street
New York, NY 10010 USA

Negative Population Growth
210 The Plaza
P.O. Box 1206,
Teaneck, NJ 07666 USA

The Pathfinder Fund
9 Galen Street, Suite 217
Watertown, MA 02172-4501 USA

Planned Parenthood Federation of America
810 7th Ave.
New York, NY 10019 USA

Population Concern
231 Tottenham Road
London W1P 9AE, U.K.

Population Crisis Committee (PCC)
1120 19th St. NW, Suite 550
Washington, D.C. 20036 USA

The Population Institute
110 Maryland Ave., NE
Washington, D.C. 20002 USA

Population Reference Bureau, Inc.
1875 Connecticut Ave. NW, Suite 520
Washington, D.C. 20009-5728 USA

Worldwatch Institute
1776 Massachusetts Ave. NW
Washington, D.C. 20036 USA

Zero Population Growth
1400 16th St. NW, 3rd Floor
Washington, D.C. 20036 USA

NATIONAL GOVERNMENTAL AGENCIES

Australian International Development Assistance Bureau
G.P.O. Box 887
Canberra, A.C.T. 2601, Australia

Canadian International Development Agency
200 Promenade du Portage, Hull
Quebec, Canada K1A 0G4

Policy Coordination Division, Economic Cooperation Bureau, Ministry of Foreign Affairs
2-2-1 Kasumigaseki, Chiyoda-ku
Tokyo, Japan

Overseas Development Administration, Health and Population Division
Eland House, Stag Place
London SW1E 5DH, U. K

U.S. Agency for International Development (U.S.A.I.D.)
Office of Population
Washington, D.C. 20523 USA

UNITED NATIONS ORGANIZATIONS

United Nations Population Fund (UNFPA)
220 East 42nd St.
New York, NY 10017 USA

World Bank
1818 H Street, NW
Washington, D.C. 20433 USA

World Health Organization (WHO)
20 Avenue Appia
1211 Geneva 27
Switzerland

Food and Agriculture Organization (FAO)
Via delle Terme di Caracalla
00100 Rome, Italy